CULTURES OF THE WORLD®

GREENLAND

David C. King

Marshall Cavendish
Benchmark

New York

PICTURE CREDITS
Cover photo: © David McLain/Getty Images
AFP: 60 • alt.TYPE/reuters: 46 • Anders Blomqvist/ Lonely Planet Images: 1, 70, 82, 93, 104, 127 • Andrew Peacock/Lonely Planet Images: 9, 50, 85, 96 • Art Directors & Trip: 10, 15, 26 • Audrius Tomonis: 135 • Besstock: 102 • Brian J. Skerry/ Getty Images: 21 • Diane Cook and Len Jenshel/ Getty Images: 116 • Ed Kashi/ Corbis: 100 • Grant Dixon/ Lonely Planet Images: 25, 111 • Hulton Archive/Getty Images: 37, 38 • KELD NAVNTOFT/AFP/Getty Images: 45 • Mansell/Time & Life Pictures/Getty Images: 30, 36 • Michael Gebicki/ Lonely Planet Images: 49 • North Wind Picture Archives: 31 • Paul Nicklen/ Getty Images: 19, 20 • photolibrary. com: 3, 4, 5, 11, 12, 14, 16, 17, 18, 22, 23, 24, 28, 34, 35, 41, 42, 43, 51, 52, 58, 62, 68, 71, 73, 78, 79, 80, 81, 83, 86, 87, 89, 90, 91, 101, 103, 108, 109, 117, 118, 120, 125, 126, 130 (RF), 131 • Pritt Vesilind/ National Geographic Images: 48 • RH Productions/ Getty Images: 6, 8 • Richard Cummings/ Lonely Planet Images: 13, 56, 75, 76 • Richard Olsenius/ Getty Images: 65 • Richard Olsenius/ National Geographic/Getty Images: 128 • SLIM ALLAGUI/AFP/Getty Images: 47, 57 • Tom Vezo/ Getty Images: 69 • Travel Ink/ Getty Images: 122 • Uriel Sinai/Getty Images: 53, 63, 77, 112 • Wolfgang Kaehler/Corbis: 55 • Yvette Cardozo/ Houserstock: 124

PRECEDING PAGE
Inuit women in their traditional folk costumes.

Publisher (U.S.): Michelle Bisson
Editors: Christine Florie, Stephanie Pee
Designer: Bernard Go Kwang Meng
Copyreader: Kristen Azzara
Cover picture researcher: Connie Gardner
Picture researcher: Thomas Khoo

Marshall Cavendish Benchmark
99 White Plains Road
Tarrytown, NY 10591
Web site: www.marshallcavendish.us

© Times Media Private Limited 1997
© Marshall Cavendish International (Asia) Private Limited 2009
All rights reserved. First edition 2009.
® "Cultures of the World" is a registered trademark of Times Publishing Limited.

Originated and designed by Times Media Private Limited
An imprint of Marshall Cavendish International (Asia) Private Limited
A member of Times Publishing Limited

All Internet sites were correct and accurate at the time of printing. All monetary figures in this publication are in U.S. dollars.

Library of Congress Cataloging-in-Publication Data
King, David C.
  Greenland / by David C. King.
    p. cm. (Cultures of the world)
  Summary: "Provides comprehensive information on the geography, history, governmental structure, economy, cultural diversity, peoples, religion, and culture of Greenland"—Provided by publisher.
  Includes bibliographical references and index.
  ISBN 978-0-7614-3118-3
1. Greenland Social life and customs. Juvenile literature. I. Title.
G750.K56 2009
998.2—dc22   2007038806

Printed in China
7 6 5 4 3 2 1

CONTENTS

Greenland's Disco Bay.

An Inuit woman in Greenland.

INTRODUCTION

GREENLAND IS THE WORLD'S LARGEST ISLAND, covering 840,000 square miles (2,175,600 sq km), making it nearly as large as Alaska and Texas combined. In spite of its great size, Greenland is one of the most sparsely populated places on Earth. More than 80 percent of the island is covered by a huge ice sheet, limiting the population of about 57,000 to living in the few ice-free regions along the coast.

Not surprisingly, much of this ice-covered island seems bleak and desolate. However, there are also areas of great beauty, including enormous glaciers and icebergs, as well as many dramatic fjords, or steep-sided inlets that wind far into the interior. There are also picturesque fishing villages with brightly colored houses. These widely scattered communities have a rich history and culture, including that of the Vikings and the Inuit. One of the most surprising features of Greenland is that a land with no cities and few people is home to a robust artistic tradition that includes art, music, and theater.

GEOGRAPHY

GREENLAND IS LOCATED BETWEEN THE North Atlantic Ocean and the Arctic Ocean, with two-thirds of the island lying within the Arctic Circle. From south to north the land stretches 1,660 miles (2,670 km), to within 500 miles (800 km) of the North Pole. In fact, Oodaaq Island, a rocky speck of land just off the northern coast, is the world's northernmost piece of land.

In geographic terms, Greenland is part of North America. Canada's Ellesmere Island is only 16 miles (26 km) to the west. The island's basic rock foundation is an extension of the Canadian Shield, which formed more than 3 billion years ago. This is different from nearby Iceland, where frequent volcanic eruptions have created some of the planet's youngest crust, while Greenland has some of the oldest rocks found in the world.

In political and historical terms, Greenland is oriented toward Europe. Greenland is not a nation; it is a self-governing territory of the small European nation of Denmark. (Greenland is 50 times larger than Denmark, but Denmark has 95 times as many people.) The nearest European country to Greenland is tiny Iceland, which lies only about 200 miles (321 km) to the southeast, across the Denmark Strait.

THE ICE SHEET

The massive ice sheet is Greenland's dominant geographic feature. Only the ice cap in Antarctica covers a greater area. The Greenland ice cap has an average depth of 5,000 feet (1,525 m) and in some places reaches a thickness of about 10,000 feet (3,050 m). With an area of 700,000 square miles (1,813,000 sq km), the ice sheet covers nearly 85 percent of the island's area. If the entire ice cap melted, the released water would raise global sea levels by more than 20 feet (6 m).

Opposite: **The ice fjord at Sermermiut, Ilulissat. Snow and ice are the dominant geographical features of Greenland.**

The inland ice cap as seen from Kangerlussuaq.

The ice cap was created over many centuries, as fallen snow became compressed into layers of ice. The weight of the ice increased steadily and became so great that the interior of the ice sheet has become pressed into a bowl-shaped depression that reaches well below sea level.

The compressed ice layers steadily push outward to the edges of the island as glaciers. Some of these glaciers move rapidly, with the front edges breaking off into the sea as icebergs. The Jakobshavn Glacier is among the fastest moving glaciers in the world, advancing as much as 100 feet (30 m) per day.

The 15 percent of the island that is not covered by ice makes up the rocky coastal areas. These coastal regions consist of numerous highlands, with mountain chains on both the east and west coasts, rising as high as 12,139 feet (3,700 m) at Gunnbjørns Feld in the southwest. The rest of the rocky crust, buried beneath the ice cap, is at or below sea level.

Along both the east and west coasts, long fjords reach far into the land, creating dramatically beautiful scenery. Sometimes glaciers fill a fjord, and then pieces break off and slide into the sea. One of the most impressive ice-packed fjords is located near Ilulissat and is a UNESCO-recognized site, which means that its preservation is considered important to the world environment.

Understanding the many features of the ice on the island and in coastal waters is vital for living in Greenland. A ship's captain or sailors in a fishing boat need to know how to navigate ice-choked harbors or coastal waters. The same is true of hunters stalking seals or whales among the ice floes and hundreds of offshore islands.

Huge blocks of ice at the mouth of the Ilulussat Jakobshavn ice fjord.

THE LANGUAGE OF ICE

The many features of Greenland's ice, and studying how those features change, has led to the creation of a special vocabulary. When inland ice comes to the edge of the island, for example, it is said to form tidewater glaciers, or glaciers that flow into the sea. At the coast, chunks of this ice are deposited directly into the water as icebergs. Technically, a chunk of ice is considered an iceberg if more than about 14 feet (5 m) of it is above the waterline. Smaller ice chunks are known as bergy bits. When less than 3 feet (1 m) is visible above the water's surface pieces are called growlers. Icebergs often contain pressurized air bubbles. On a summer day with warm sunshine, these bubbles often explode, creating a shower of fragments called brash ice.

Sea ice is different; it is frozen seawater that first forms small, plate-shaped crystals called frazil ice. These crystals coagulate into a stewlike mixture known as grease ice. The grease ice can remain in slushy lumps called shugas or can coagulate further into a thin crust, or nilas, which is often transparent, or else into larger circular plates known as pancake ice. Finally, sea ice may thicken to as much as 9 feet (3 m), forming pack ice (*above*).

Pack ice is always in motion, and it can break up into flat-topped pieces called ice floes. The areas of open water between floes are known as leads or polynyas. Some of the openings are permanent, such as the North Water Polynya, a large area between Greenland and Ellesmere Island. Other leads are open in summer but freeze up in winter. Polynyas stay open in areas where swift ocean currents flow over shallow water, preventing the ice from freezing. Polar bears and seals are frequently found on large floes, and both whales and seals often travel through polynyas. Inuit hunters traditionally have stalked these areas in search of their prey.

LAND AND SEA

Most of Greenland is constantly covered by ice, and it is also surrounded by ice. Ocean currents keep the sea ice in motion. This movement helps determine where people live and also contributes to making the coastal waters ideal for fishing.

Two major currents flow around the island, pushing icebergs and the various forms of sea ice. The East Greenland Current flows from the Arctic south along the island's east coast. The pack ice becomes so thick, up to 15 feet (4.6 m), that ships cannot reach this coast. The temperature decrease in the Arctic waters and the pack-ice barrier combine to make the entire east side of the island inhospitable to humans. Not surprisingly, the east coast is home to few people and only two towns. The entire northeastern quarter of the island is covered by Northeast Greenland National Park, the largest national park in the world.

As the current rounds the southern tip of Greenland at Uummannarsuaq (also known as Cape Farewell), it meets a portion of the warm Gulf Stream current. The collision of these currents stirs the waters, creating a nutrient-rich stew perfect for supporting numerous tiny plants and animals. Millions of fish are drawn to the tasty feeding ground that fills the area between southern Greenland and Canada's Baffin Island. Fishing boats from several countries join in.

The presence of krill in the waters off Greenland attract millions of fish, which has resulted in a booming fishing industry.

The warmed current rounds Cape Farewell and flows north as the West Greenland Current. Because the water is warmer than on the opposite coast, western Greenland is much more inviting to humans, and the coastal waters are generally ice free.

The movements of the many ice forms are tracked by the Danish Meteorological Institute (DMI) to aid in navigation. Frequent reports are issued, giving estimates of ice-floe density and areas of open water.

CLIMATE

Greenland has a bleak Arctic climate that is softened slightly in the southwest by the edge of the Gulf Stream current. Average January temperatures range from 21°F (−6°C) in the south to −31°F (−35°C) in the north. Along the southwest coast, summer temperatures average 45° F (7°C), and in the north the average is 39°F (4°C). The island receives

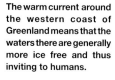

The warm current around the western coast of Greenland means that the waters there are generally more ice free and thus inviting to humans.

little precipitation, except in the south. The north receives only about 2 inches (5 cm) per year, about the same amount as a desert climate.

The island often experiences rapid changes from sunshine to blinding blizzards that are caused by the movement of low-pressure air masses over the permanent layer of cold air that hovers above the interior ice cap. Winds of 100 miles (160 km) per hour in the north are not uncommon.

Because of the tilt of Earth's axis and Greenland's proximity to the North Pole, most of the island experiences long periods of sunshine in the summer and equally long periods in winter when the sun does not rise at all. The periods of "midnight sun" and continual darkness lengthen depending on a location's proximity to the North Pole.

A village in Nanortalik. Settlements in Greenland have been determined mainly by climate and geography.

Over the past 30 years, concerns about climate change, specifically global warming, have focused world attention on Greenland. Researchers report a shocking increase in the speed of the melting of the island's ice cap and in the movement of glaciers. These changes provide scientists with dramatic evidence of the warming of the planet's climate.

SETTLEMENT PATTERNS

The features of Greenland's climate and landforms have helped determine the island's settlement patterns. Nearly all of the island's roughly 57,000 inhabitants live on the west coast, especially near the southern tip. Most families live in small cottages perched on the rocky coast. There are also a few larger towns where small packing plants ship

AURORA BOREALIS

One of the most striking features of Greenland, and other Arctic regions as well, is the phenomenon called the aurora borealis or northern lights. Throughout history, people have tried to explain the vivid curtains of color that glow with eerie beauty in the night sky. According to Inuit legend, the lights represent Inuit ancestors dancing in the heavens. Other Arctic peoples have had other explanations. In Scandinavian folklore, for instance, the northern lights were said to be the resting place of deceased, unmarried women.

Modern science has a found less romantic explanation that involves solar winds, which create a stream of particles from the sun that collide with oxygen and hydrogen atoms in Earth's upper atmosphere. These collisions produce the magenta and green waves of the northern lights as Earth's magnetic field draws the particles toward the polar regions.

crabs, shrimp, halibut, and other fish to Denmark. There are no cities. In fact, the population of the entire island is about the same as that of a small American city, such as Albany, Georgia.

The coastline is broken up into hundreds of inlets, coves, bays, and fjords. Because of these indentations, the coastline of this island is longer than that of the United States. This long coast provides a dramatic way of considering Greenland's size: traveling around Earth at the equator, the distance—24,430 miles (39,315 km)—would be about the same as if traveling all the way around Greenland, including all the inlets.

The population of Greenland is a mixture of Danish and Inuit, with the Inuit making up about 80 percent of the total. The majority of the people have always eked out a livelihood by hunting whales, seals, and land animals and by fishing the coastal waters.

Although Greenland is smaller than the United States, it has a longer coastline.

The musk ox is native to Greenland, feeding mainly on ground plants, such as grasses and sedges.

MUSK OXEN

Greenland's harsh environment means it has sparse wildlife, although what does exist is distinctive and intriguing. The musk ox is a good example. This shaggy animal, weighing about 650 pounds (295 kg), looks like a stout, wooly bison, although it is actually more closely related to the goat. Musk oxen are vegetarians and quite passive. Inuit hunters found them to be easy prey and a good source of meat. In the west of the island they were hunted almost to extinction. Musk oxen were relocated there from the east and have thrived in their new home. Musk oxen have two coats; the inner coat is soft and thick, while the outer coat is coarse and grows through the thick inner coat. The inner coat is used to make yarn for clothing.

OTHER MAMMALS

The favorite prey of hunters is the caribou, known as reindeer in Scandinavian countries. Caribou are plentiful wherever there is open land,

and in autumn it seems that everyone in Greenland drops everything to hunt them. There are also a few ranches where these majestic animals are raised for their meat and fur.

The lumbering giant of this frozen land is the polar bear. This great animal, which can actually move with surprising speed, is well adapted to the environment. In addition to its thick coat and snow-white coloring, it also has a second set of eyelids that protects it from snow blindness and acts as swim goggles when the bears swim underwater. Most polar bears live in the far northeast, hundreds of miles from human settlements. Only few drift south on ice floes, so hunters usually have to travel far to obtain this prey.

The recent environmental changes in Greenland and the Arctic have reduced the polar bear population. It is hoped that new restrictions

Environmental changes, such as global warming, have reduced the polar bear population.

on hunting will help it recover, but their situation reflects the serious environmental issues facing Greenland and other arctic regions.

Several of Greenland's mammals have the advantage of white fur to camouflage them in the snow. The fur of arctic foxes, for example, is blue gray in the summer months, but turns white in the winter. The same type of color change serves the arctic hare.

The small, mouse-sized lemming is the smallest mammal in Greenland. Lemmings are noted for "mass suicides," as thousands have been known to rush over cliffs into the sea. However, scientists report that overpopulation sends them on a frantic search for food, and many are pushed into the sea; it does not seem to be a deliberate suicide.

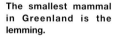

The smallest mammal in Greenland is the lemming.

WHALES AND WALRUSES

Throughout history the hunting of whales has been the major occupation of the Inuit. Traditionally, they hunted in kayaks using simple harpoons. Bowhead whales were a favorite to hunt for meat, bone, and oil. The bowheads were big, up to 65 feet (20 m) in length, and slow moving, making them easy to hunt. Beluga whales were also popular and were said to provide the tastiest meat. Other whales hunted by the Inuit included small minke whales, killer whales, and the large humpback whales.

One of the most unusual whales hunted by the Inuit is the narwhal, with its unique spiral tusk that is actually an unusual tooth. This remarkable creature was viewed in Medieval Europe as proof that the mythical unicorn actually existed. In many European countries during the Middle Ages, narwhal teeth were worth 20 times their weight in gold.

Two narwhals lock tusks as they surface from the water to take a breath.

Overhunting of walruses for their prized tusks and meat have seen them placed under protection since 1972.

The overhunting of whales by countries throughout the world brought many whale species close to extinction. This prompted vigorous international efforts to outlaw the hunting of whales. Exceptions to these restrictions were granted to the Inuit because their way of life has been dependent on traditional hunting. The large whaling nations also admitted that the limited take of the Inuit could not be blamed for the population declines.

Walruses, with their perfect-for-carving tusks and comical beards, were once quite common in Greenland, but they were hunted to the edge of extinction throughout the Arctic for both their meat and tusks. They have been protected worldwide since 1972, although Greenlanders still have the right to hunt a few each year. The most productive area for walrus hunters is in Northeast Greenland National Park.

SEALS, FISH, AND BIRD LIFE

Seals are the most common of Greenland's mammals and were a major source of food and other materials for Greenlanders. Ringed seals grow to be nearly 5 feet (1.5 m) long and weigh about 150 pounds (70 kg). Young ringed seals remain on the ice until they are nearly grown, which makes them easy prey.

Harp seals like to bask on ice, a habit that gave them their scientific name: *Pagophilus groenlandicus* (Greenland's ice lovers). Found throughout the Arctic, they are famous for the snow-white fur of their young. This coat lasts only a few weeks, but that is long enough to cause a flurry of hunting, especially in eastern Canada.

These seals, along with the less-common bearded seals and hooded seals, were once central to the Greenlandic economy. All parts of the

An adult harp seal with her young.

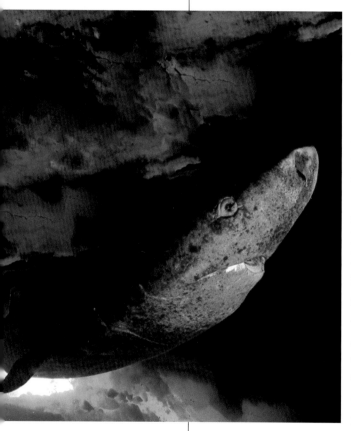

The greenland shark is native to arctic waters. It has an acute sense of smell that helps it in catching prey.

animal were used, including the blubber, which was used for lamp oil. However, the wasteful practice in North America, especially Newfoundland, of clubbing baby seals for their fur led to a worldwide demand to stop the practice. By the 1990s the demand for sealskins had dropped sharply. Around 2003, however, demand picked up, and hunters again receive a decent return for each skin.

Fish are abundant in both Greenland's fresh and saltwater, although overfishing has led to dangerously low levels of cod, Atlantic halibut, and scallops—three popular species for commercial fishing. However, the lakes and streams still have abundant populations of Arctic char, a troutlike fish. In addition, outstanding Atlantic salmon and redfish are valuable, along with shrimp, snow crab, and a species of halibut. The Greenland shark, found in most Arctic waters, grows to about 21 feet (6.4 m) in length. It is hunted for its liver oil.

Birds are not as plentiful in Greenland as they are in milder climates, but about 50 hardy species nest along its shores. Another 150 species migrate across the island, including such common varieties as northern wheateaters, black-and-white snow buntings, and noisy, coal black ravens. Peregrine falcons and gyrfalcons are rarer visitors to Greenland, and the snowy owl spends all but the coldest months on the northern tundra.

The most common seabirds are Iceland gulls, terns, skuas, and kittiwakes.

PENGUIN LOOK-ALIKES

Several bird species have features that are easily confused with those of true penguins. The popular puffin (*below*), for example, with its thick orange bill, looks very penguinlike, and stuffed puffin toys are popular souvenirs.

Puffins are relatives of the now-extinct great auk. Sixteenth-century explorers first spotted the big bird, about 2 feet (61 cm) tall, and gave it the name penguin ("whitehead"). Years later, when the birds now identified as penguins were seen in the Southern Hemisphere, the name penguin was applied to them as well. Would the great auk still be called a penguin today? Probably not, although like penguins, it could not fly. But the question was rendered moot when the auk became extinct in around 1850, following years of vigorous overhunting of the meaty, easy-to-catch bird.

Dovekies look like small penguins, but their ability to fly immediately excludes them from the penguin category. True penguins live only in the Southern Hemisphere, they do not fly, they have webbed feet, and their wings act more like flippers than any aid to flight.

Farther north, above Disco Bay, fulmars, puffins, and ptarmigans are common. In higher wetland areas, red-necked phalarope and snow geese, including one called the Greenland white-fronted goose, spend summers on the island. Several species of sea ducks nest there, too, including eider ducks, one of the largest ducks in the Northern Hemisphere.

PLANT LIFE

Three Greenland white-fronted geese in flight. These geese spend their summers on Greenland.

The climate of Greenland and the enormous ice sheet place severe limitations on the island's plant life. On the roughly 15 percent of the island that is clear of snow during the summer, only the top few feet of soil thaw. Beneath that layer, the ground remains frozen and is called permafrost.

Most of the soil above the permafrost remains swamplike because the water in it cannot sink through the ice. This type of environment is called tundra.

During the short growing season with its almost constant sunshine, the tundra bursts into color. Nearly 250 species of plants grow, including a variety of colorful flowers: yellow-petaled arctic poppies, hawkweeds, and clumps of edible blue violet arctic harebell. One of the most popular plants is Greenland's national flower, the broad-leaved fireweed, which bursts into a large red blossom with dark red or purple veins. The Inuit call it *niviarsiaq* ("young woman"); it is also known as large-flowered rosebay or French willow.

Greenlanders also look forward to several varieties of berries. These include mountainside clusters of crowberries and arctic bilberries, better known to North Americans as blackberries and blueberries. Their leaves turn a beautiful russet or dull red, creating magnificent hillside carpets.

Greenland is north of the timberline, the place where the climate becomes too cold for trees to grow. The island does have dwarf-size clusters of willow and birch. However, these plants look more like small shrubs or bushes than true trees.

Greenland's national flower, the broad-leaved fireweed, also known as *niviarsiaq*.

25

HISTORY

FOR MOST OF HISTORY, Greenland was largely unknown to the rest of the world. The vast, ice-covered land was not discovered by Europeans until the 10th century A.D. The first European settlement was started by the Norse (or Vikings) in 986 A.D. It lasted barely 500 years before the settlers mysteriously disappeared. Before the Norse, different groups of Inuit had eked out an existence at different times, but they, too, disappeared before modern Greenland began to emerge as a combination of Inuit and European peoples, about 600 years ago.

Opposite: **The ruins of ancient dwellings of the Saqqaq culture.**

EARLY INUIT CULTURES

At different times over a 3,000-year period, Inuit groups established settlements on the island. None of the groups left written records, but archaeologists have been able to piece together a fairly clear picture of each group's way of life.

Each culture is identified by the location of its major settlement. The first group, for example, is known as Independence I because of its location at Independence Sound in Peary Land. This group of no more than 500 Inuit crossed over from the island of Ellesmere around 2400 B.C. They had a simple way of life, surviving in the harsh environment by hunting and fishing with Stone Age technology. The climate at that time was warmer than it is today, so the Independence I people were able to fish even in the northern fjords. Archaeological evidence shows that their technology included kayaks and bone needles for sewing clothing, and probably tents. After about 500 years the Independence I culture vanished. They may have been absorbed by another society or may have migrated back to the west, to Canada or Alaska.

At about the same time another group, called the Saqqaq culture, arrived on the west coast of Greenland, where they spread out over a wide area around Disco Bay. Known as Independence II, the Saqqaq culture had a more advanced technology and survived roughly 1,000 years.

A third group, known as the Dorset culture, probably emerged from the Saqqaq around 500 B.C. The Dorset people developed the technology to hunt sea mammals—seals and walruses—using large, open boats called umiaks, made of tough sealskin. They also extracted oil from seal and whale blubber, which provided them with fuel to create light and heat through the cold, dark winter nights. Archaeological evidence also indicates their skill in carving small figures of humans and animals out of bone, ivory, and caribou antler.

Around 900 A.D. a new group—the Thule culture—migrated from Alaska, probably following the migration of bowhead whales. They intermingled with the Dorset people, and the two groups formed a

An Inuit sits, watching the sea, in an umiak.

vigorous new culture; the Thule are the ancestors of the modern Inuit of Greenland and Canada. The Thule used kayaks and umiaks for hunting, and on land they used dogsleds and bows and arrows.

During the 12th century the climate entered a dramatic cooling trend that splintered the Thule into small groups and pushed them south along both coasts. By the time these subgroups met again, at the southern tip of Greenland, they could hardly understand each other's language.

THE NORSE PERIOD

About 930 A.D. a Viking explorer named Gunnbjörn Ulfsson was on a ship that was blown off course. He accidentally came upon the great island, becoming the first European to see it. (To honor Ulfsson, the highest peak on the island was later named after him.)

Another 50 years passed before anyone followed up on Ulfsson's discovery. In the year 982 a courageous explorer named Erik Thorvaldsson—better known as Erik the Red—was forced to leave his homeland of Iceland after being found guilty of manslaughter in a revenge killing. For the next three years Erik and a handful of followers explored the coasts of Greenland.

LEIF ERIKSSON

In 1001 Erik the Red's son Leif Eriksson sailed south from Greenland in search of lumber needed for the construction of boats and homes. He and his crew landed in Newfoundland, naming it Vinland, and spent the winter there. Many believe they were the first Europeans to set foot on the North American continent. Leif had earlier played a leading role in bringing Christianity to Greenland.

Erik tried returning to Iceland, assuming his exile was over. When he found that he was still not welcome there, he decided to start a settlement on Greenland. To attract colonists, he called the island Greenland, hoping the name would conjure up images of green forests and fertile farm fields. His promotional scheme worked: In the summer of 986 he set sail for Greenland, leading 25 ships loaded with prospective settlers and their supplies, including livestock. It was a hard crossing, however, because of ice and storms, and 11 of the ships were lost or turned back.

The Vikings, who were also known as the Norse or Norsemen, after their original homeland of Norway, were fortunate to arrive at a time when Greenland's climate was entering a long warm spell. They started two settlements, both on the west coast, establishing farms along the banks of the fjords. Gradually the two communities became known as the Eastern and Western Settlements.

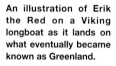

An illustration of Erik the Red on a Viking longboat as it lands on what eventually became known as Greenland.

The Norse settlements prospered for a time, with between 3,000 and 5,000 people living on about 400 farms at the colony's peak. They raised the cattle, sheep, and other livestock they had brought with them, and they supplemented their diet by sending hunting parties north along the coast and into the interior. The hunters brought back seal meat and skins, caribou, musk ox, and occasionally whale meat (from a whale that had been beached, since the Norse were not skilled whalers). They also traded with Norway and other European countries, exchanging ivory from walrus tusks, seals, sheep's wool, sheepskins, and cattle hides in exchange for iron tools and wood.

A fleet of Viking ships at sea. The Vikings from Norway eventually formed two settlements on the east and west of Greenland.

CHRISTIANITY AND THE COOLING CLIMATE

The Norse settlers followed the traditional Norse religion, which worshipped many gods, such as Thor, the god of thunder. Soon after their arrival, they were converted to Christianity and, in the early 12th century, they petitioned the king of Norway to establish a bishopric, or administrative unit overseen by a bishop, in Greenland, accompanying their appeal with elaborate gifts, including walrus tusks, whalebone, and a pair of polar bear cubs. A Swedish monk named Arnold was named bishop in 1124, and a handsome red sandstone church was built at Gardar (now Igaliku). Several churches were built in other villages as well.

Over the next century the church exercised increasing power over the Norse community. It punished troublemakers and usually took over their livestock or their land. In 1261, when Norway annexed Greenland, much of the land was already controlled by the church. (Iceland accepted the rule of the Norwegian king at the same time.) The Norwegian king established a trade monopoly, allowing only his ships to bring supplies to and from Greenland.

The settlements might have continued to prosper under Norwegian rule, but climate change probably doomed the colony. A dramatic cooling trend that began in the late 13th century created havoc for the settlers. Livestock began to freeze, the wool industry failed, and crops no longer grew. The coastal ice pack thickened, making it increasingly difficult for ships to bring supplies.

WHAT HAPPENED TO THE NORSE?

In about 1350 the settlers abandoned the Western Settlement, which was the warmer of the two. The Norse clung to the Eastern Settlement for a few more years. In 1392 a powerful trade group in northern Europe called the Hanseatic League destroyed Bergen, the one port in Norway from which ships officially allowed to trade with Greenland sailed, leaving the island completely isolated from the outside world. In 1408 an Icelander reported attending a wedding at one of the Norse communities. That 1408 report was the last official news about the Norse of Greenland.

There are several theories about what happened to the Norse settlers, but none have been proven. Some historians think that the climate was simply too cold for the settlers to survive, so they moved away, perhaps back to Iceland. A second theory is that a new species of caterpillar invaded the island and destroyed the plants on which their livestock depended. Other theories suggest that the Norse were absorbed into Inuit cultures or that the Black Death, which was sweeping through much of Europe, may have somehow reached Greenland. Although theories continue to emerge now and then, the fate of the Norse Greenland settlers remains a mystery.

THE LAST INUIT MIGRATIONS

In 1818 the explorer John Ross found a small band of Inuit who called themselves the Polar Inuit, or Inughuit. They lived a simple life, apparently isolated from other Inuit groups. They no longer used bows and arrows or kayaks, so their prey was limited to mammals that climbed up on the ice, such as seals and walruses.

About 40 years after Ross's visit, the last Inuit migration to Greenland took place, when another group migrated from Canada across Baffin Island and Ellesmere Island to northern Greenland. They helped the Inughuit relearn to use the kayak and bows and arrows.

The Inughuit later helped explorers search for routes to the North Pole. Today they are regarded as the best resource for restoring Inuit traditions in hunting, fishing, and daily living.

The Norse did leave behind tantalizing reminders of their five centuries on Greenland. Ruins of churches and other buildings are scattered among the villages of southern Greenland.

NEW EUROPEAN INTERESTS

In the 16th century, Europe launched a search for sea routes to the spices and wealth of Eastern Asia (China, India, and Indonesia). The voyages of Christopher Columbus were part of that search. So were the many expeditions searching for a Northwest Passage—a sea route through or north of the North American continent. Such a sea route would reduce the time required to reach Asia, as the main route went all the way around Africa and across the Indian Ocean, and another went all the way around South America.

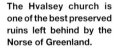

The Hvalsey church is one of the best preserved ruins left behind by the Norse of Greenland.

This search for a Northwest Passage continued on and off from the mid-1500s through the 1700s. One of the most important of these efforts was led by the English explorer Martin Frobisher, who spent three years in the 1570s searching the uncharted waters around Greenland and the Canadian Arctic. Frobisher and his crew could not get through the ice pack to reach the coast of Greenland, and they failed to find the Northwest Passage.

Other explorers followed, including Henry Hudson and John Davis, who made several trips, starting in 1585, during which he made accurate maps of Greenland's west coast. He also made friends with the Inuit and wrote the first ethnographic, geographic, and biologic reports on the people.

Ice like this often blocks and renders the Northwest passage impassable.

Opposite: **King Christian IV (1577–1648), of Denmark claimed Greenland for Denmark.**

THE ELUSIVE NORTH POLE

The search for the North Pole reached a fever pitch in the late 19th and early 20th centuries, when 17 separate expeditions failed to reach the pole. The quest seemed to be over when a determined American explorer—Robert E. Peary (*below*) (1865–1920)—announced in 1909 that he had reached the pole with a 22-man expedition, including the African-American explorer Matthew Henson.

Peary had single-mindedly worked toward that goal since 1886, when he first traveled to Greenland. From 1893 to 1909 he made several futile attempts to reach the pole, losing eight toes to frostbite in the process. Then, in 1908, he allowed his ship to be frozen into the Arctic ice for four months before making his final dash. On April 6, 1909, he placed an American flag in the ice at the map coordinates for the pole.

Peary was hailed as a great hero, but his claim was quickly challenged by another explorer, who also had no good way to prove his claim. Two later studies concluded that the claims of both American explorers were fraudulent. In 1983 the First International Congress on the North Pole was kinder to Peary, concluding that there was not enough evidence to support his claim. The first explorer with solid evidence that he had reached the pole was another American, Ralph Plaisted, who reached the pole by snowmobile in 1968.

Another European development had an impact on Greenlandic life: In the mid-1600s, whaling ships from Norway, England, Scotland, and the Netherlands began arriving in Greenland in steadily increasing numbers. The whaling crews generally stayed on their ships, but there was a good deal of trade and social mixing as well. The Inuit were particularly eager to obtain knives and other items made of iron. The Europeans, in turn, were interested in ivory, especially the spiral tusks of the narwhal. Many Europeans believed these tusks to be the horns of the mythical unicorn. The hunting of these marine mammals took a heavy toll on their population by the late 19th century.

DENMARK TAKES CONTROL

Denmark sent several expeditions to discover the fate of the Norse settlers, but without success. King Christian IV used the 1605 expedition to claim all of Greenland for Denmark. Norway disputed the claim, based on its whaling history, but its claim was rejected as recently as 1933.

A century later, in 1721, Pastor Hans Egede received permission to establish a Lutheran mission and trading post in Greenland. His hope of finding descendants of the Norse settlers failed, so he turned his attention to converting the Inuit to Christianity.

GREENLAND'S GREATEST HERO

Knud Rasmussen was born in Greenland in 1879 of mixed Danish, Norwegian, and Inuit descent. After completing his education in Denmark, he tried a variety of careers, including medicine and opera singing, before finding his true calling as a writer for a 1902 Danish expedition to northwestern Greenland.

Rasmussen became fascinated with the Inuit people and their way of life. With another Arctic explorer and writer, Peter Freuchen, he started a trading company on North Star Bay. It was located at Thule, and it was successful enough to fund four more expeditions to explore Greenland.

During these expeditions Rasmussen lived with the Inuit, shared their food, hunted with them, and wrote copiously about their way of life. His books provide a unique and detailed record of societies that have since disappeared. He also made a film called *Paolo's Wedding*, using Inuits as actors. It

was released in 1936 and provides an unusual documentary of Greenland and the life of the indigenous people.

Rasmussen remains a national hero today. After he died of food poisoning in 1933, the northern part of the island was named in his honor.

Over the following century, Christian missionaries and Danish government officials imposed a series of rules that impacted Inuit life. The church outlawed the Inuit's traditional religious practices, including drumming, which had been used to tame the spirits that were believed to reside in all animals and objects. The new rules encouraged the people to live in nuclear families rather than communally. A number of researchers feel that these changes undermined the Inuit's sense of social cohesion, even ending certain organizations that had been important to their sense of belonging, such as a food-sharing system.

The Danish government also imposed a trade monopoly in 1774, placing the Royal Greenland Trade Department (KGH, for its name in Danish) in charge. As Inuits developed a taste for such KGH "luxuries" as tobacco and coffee, they became less interested in following their traditional nomadic lifestyle, preferring instead to settle more permanently near the trading posts.

RECENT HISTORY

In September 1939 the German dictator Adolf Hitler plunged the world into World War II (1939–1945). With frightening speed, German troops stormed across Europe, occupying country after country, including Denmark. Even though the United States did not enter the war until December 1941, American forces had already set up several air bases, including one at Thule, and also a small naval base at Green Valley (Gronnedal). It was vital to the United States and its allies that American forces be able to ship supplies, including aircraft, to England and other friendly nations.

The people of Greenland took advantage of the absence of Denmark's government to take some matters into their own hands. They knew how vital accurate weather reporting was for ocean vessels and bomber aircraft, so they set up a series of small weather stations on the east coast of the island. They also organized a partly armed military force to watch for German attempts to land on the coast.

A series of small but heroic battles developed when sparse German forces tried to set up their own weather stations on the coast or on offshore islands. On several occasions fighting erupted, and while several Greenlanders were killed, the Germans suffered more casualties and several became prisoners of the United States.

In the early years of the war German submarines terrorized the North Atlantic. The subs, or U-boats, downed dozens of ships, including those carrying vitally important warplanes. To make delivery to England safer, Americans began flying the new aircraft to their base at Thule, where they were refueled and then flown to northern England.

After the war, Denmark renewed its interest in Greenland. The government tried to impose a new, more modern way of life on the Greenlanders. The island was made a county of Denmark in 1953, and Greenlanders were granted full Danish citizenship. Following the kind of social engineering that was common in the 1950s, the Danes moved people out of their huts and resettled them in apartment buildings. Smaller villages were considered impractical, so their residents were moved to larger regional centers. Many were put to work in the new cod-processing plants.

After a few years of modest success the experiment gradually crumbled. Most Inuit hated being removed from their lands, and alcoholism became a problem. In the 1980s climate change forced the cod to move away from the island. The fish-processing plants closed, and unemployment became widespread.

Throughout the years of Danish modernizing, Greenlanders agitated for more control over their own affairs. In 1978 Greenlandic independence was approved, and the island became mostly independent. Denmark, however, maintains control over Greenland's defense and its international relations. While Greenlanders would like still more control, they continue to remain dependent on Danish subsidies.

An aerial view of the U.S. air base at Thule.

41

GOVERNMENT

ALTHOUGH DENMARK HAD CLAIMED Greenland in 1605, the Danes allowed the Inuit to manage their own affairs. Family, clan, and tribal groups based their rules on long-standing traditions and customs. The most visible evidence of the Danish presence was the Danish Christianizing missions and the trading stations established by the Royal Greenland Trade Department (KGH).

In the 1950s the Danish government launched a modernization program. The program forced many Inuits to abandon their traditional hunting and fishing villages and to move into the towns to work at jobs in government-operated fish-processing plants.

Greenlanders protested against many of the changes, including living in new, modern housing that seemed impersonal and sterile compared to their traditional homes. In 1953 the government passed a Home Rule provision, changing the constitution to make Greenland a county of

Left: **Relocation policies by the government left many villages deserted, like this one at Kangerq.**

Opposite: **The flag of Greenland.**

Opposite: **Queen Margrethe of Denmark (*right*), wears a traditional Inuit outfit during the celebration of the 25th anniversary of Greenland's home rule.**

Denmark and granting Greenlanders all the rights of Danish citizenship. Home Rule eased the tensions between Denmark and Greenlanders, but some people began to think that they would better off with greater independence from Denmark.

In 1973 the Danish people approved a referendum to join the European Economic Community (now called the EU). Greenland became part of the referendum even though 70 percent of the Greenlanders voted against it. They disliked the referendum because they feared it would lead to an invasion of Greenland's prime fishing waters by European fishing trawlers.

Their fears were well founded. Almost immediately, the fish-laden waters off Greenland's coasts became clogged with fishing boats from England, Germany, and other countries vying for cod, halibut, and other prized commercial fish. Greenlanders protested, and the Danish government relented by allowing them to begin running their own affairs. A Home Rule law enabled Greenland to set up its own government and also allowed Greenland to send two representatives to the Danish parliament, or Folketing.

The trade organization—KGH—that had run trade matters for several centuries was replaced by the Kalaallit Niuerfiat (KNI), which began handling the importation of supplies and managing the island's infrastructure.

Greenland would now have its own parliament—the Landstinget—and a prime minister, giving its people control over most matters of government. Denmark continued to manage national defense and some aspects of international trade. In 1985 Greenland revealed its greater independence when a new fisheries agreement was reached, allowing Greenland to withdraw from the EEC while still remaining part of Denmark.

The anti-Danish feeling on the part of some Greenlanders continued through the 1980s. Schools began teaching Greenlandic rather than Danish, and people spoke quietly of moving toward complete independence. Most Greenlanders realize that a complete break is unrealistic, because the island continues to depend heavily on financial subsidies from Denmark. Nevertheless, the leading political party in 2007, called Siumut, which means "the forward party," continues to press for greater independence from Denmark. And the smaller Inuit party still argues that complete independence is attainable.

THE STRUCTURE OF THE GOVERNMENT

The government of Greenland is a parliamentary democracy within a constitutional monarchy. The official head of state is the king or queen of Denmark. Since 1972 the head of state has been Queen Margrethe II. The entire royal family is very popular among Greenlanders, and none more so than their beloved Queen Margrethe. The queen appoints a high commissioner to represent her in Greenland. The commissioner oversees elections, reviews matters of state and family law, and considers any matters that might affect Denmark.

The legislative branch of Greenland's Home Rule Government is a unicameral (one-house) parliament, the Landstinget. It has 31 seats elected by proportional representation (that is, larger parties have more seats). The legislators are elected to four-year terms.

The executive branch is headed by the prime minister, who is elected by the Landstinget. The Parliament appoints a small board, or committee, of between two and six members to form the Landsstyre—the Home Rule Cabinet. The Landsstyre conducts the day-to-day business of the government.

The judicial branch consists of several district courts, in which most cases are tried. Appeals can be made to a high court, or Landsret. Decisions made by the Landsret can also be appealed further to the Østre Landsret (or Eastern Division) of the Supreme Court, in Copenhagen.

Greenland's former prime minister Jonathan Motzfeldt (*left*) presents Denmark's crown prince Frederik with a polar bear claw.

There are no prisons in Greenland; when necessary, prisoners are taken to Denmark.

With its greater degree of independence under the Home Rule Law, Greenlanders consider their island to be an Inuit nation. Most Danish place names have been replaced by Inuit names. The center of Danish civilization on the island—Godthaab—is now called Nuuk.

Local government is divided into three large districts called Landsdele. There are 18 municipalities within Greenland, with a mayor and district council serving four-year terms.

International relations involve the Home Rule Government in certain ways. After leaving the EU, Greenland signed a special treaty with the Union, exempting it from EU requirements but allowing it to remain part of Denmark. The government has also started several smaller organizations to work cooperatively with both Iceland and the Faroe Islands, and with the Inuit populations of Canada and Russia. In 1996 Greenland also became one of the founders of the environmental Arctic Council.

Originally called by its Danish name, Godthaab, the city center of Greenland is now known by its Inuit name of Nuuk.

ECONOMY

CONTACT WITH WESTERN NATIONS has had a profound impact on the native peoples of Greenland and other Arctic regions. On the surface life in many Inuit towns and villages resembles that of communities throughout the Western world—people have satellite TV, Internet access, well-stocked stores, and a few modern vehicles. Beneath the surface, however, the hunting and foraging traditions that have been in place for centuries remain strong and highly valued. And the most admired groups in Greenland are the Inughuit of northern Greenland who continue to live the traditional hunting lifestyle.

For most Greenlanders today life involves a constant struggle with forces that they cannot control—forces that include environmental changes as well as technological innovations introduced by industrialized nations, such as Denmark and the United States. The result of these changes has been

Left: **Many households in Greenland now have access to satellite TV.**

Opposite: **Inuit on a fishing boat. A large proportion of Greenlanders are engaged in the fishing industry.**

years of upheaval, as Greenlanders search to find a balance between the innovations of modern life and the traditions and customs they cherish. Faced with many uncertainties, some people have succumbed to despair and depression, but a growing number have become determined to take greater control of their present and future.

THE IMPACT OF CLIMATE CHANGE

Less than 1 percent of the island's vast land area is suitable for farming. Only a handful of crops can be grown, and even these require help from greenhouses early in their growing season. With almost no agriculture, the Inuit traditionally relied on hunting to provide meat, skins for clothing and for making kayaks, and fat for fuel. They also sold sealskins, which provided vital supplies of money.

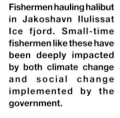

Fishermen hauling halibut in Jakoshavn Ilulissat Ice fjord. Small-time fishermen like these have been deeply impacted by both climate change and social change implemented by the government.

There was no scarcity of sea mammals and other animals to hunt. Seals were by far their primary prey, but there were also walruses, occasional whales, and polar bears, prized for their meat and their thick pelts. In the autumn the Inuit moved inland to hunt caribou both for its meat and its antlers.

Around 1900, however, a change in climate had a devastating effect on this way of life. The seas around Greenland rapidly grew warmer, and the seals migrated north, to colder waters. As the sea mammals moved away, cod, salmon, halibut, and other fish moved into the region. With the assistance and financial aid of the Danish government, the Inuit turned from seal hunting to commercial fishing. With processing plants established in several towns, commercial fishing quickly became a mainstay of the economy.

The Inuit hunt caribou for its meat and antlers.

Greenlanders were moved out of their traditional housing into apartment blocks like this one.

When the first fish-processing plant was built at Sisimiut in the mid-1920s, shrimp boats flocked to the harbor, and Sisimiut soon became the island's second largest town. Today, a company known as Royal Greenland controls the fishing industry, which now employs several thousand people. Shrimp is currently the main catch, amounting to nearly 80,000 tons a year. While cod have nearly disappeared, halibut has become an important export product.

THE LIMITS OF GOVERNMENT ACTIONS

Some of the Danish government's efforts to improve Greenland's economy did not work as planned. In 1953, for example, when Greenlanders were given full Danish citizenship, the government tried to modernize the towns for greater efficiency. Hundreds of traditional sod huts were torn down, and their residents were moved into long, low, dull-looking apartment buildings, each housing about 15 families. Some smaller villages were considered too inefficient to modernize, so the inhabitants were sent to relocation centers, where there was the promise of factory jobs.

The transitions proved difficult for many Inuit. They were not accustomed to town life. They missed their traditional activities—hunting, kayaking, and visiting with neighbors. In many towns there were not enough jobs, and unemployment became a nagging problem, the unemployment rate hovering around 10 percent.

THE IMPACT OF SOCIAL CHANGE

For many years the Inughuit and other Inuit groups carried on a lively trade in sealskins, for which there was a great demand in Europe and the Americas. Over the past 50 or 60 years, however, worldwide attitudes have changed regarding the importing and sale of animal skins and furs.

Many Inuit had to relocate and take up factory jobs, such as this man working at a fish processing plant in Ilulissat.

53

The overhunting of whales, seals, walruses, and other sea mammals led to shocking reductions in their populations, bringing some species to the brink of extinction. By the 1990s many countries and several international organizations had instituted strict bans on the harvesting or importing of many species.

The traditional Inughuit economy suffered heavy losses. The inability to sell sealskins was particularly frustrating because Greenland had no shortage of seals, especially ringed seals and harp seals, two species whose populations still numbered in the millions. The hunters had always been proud of the fact that they hunted not only for the skins; they used virtually every part of the animal—the meat for food, the pelts for clothing and for bench coverings in their homes, the blubber for oil to use for heat and light, and other parts for household items.

The ban on selling sealskins has been modified recently, which has enabled a number of villages to recover economically. Designers in fashion centers such as Paris and New York began purchasing more sealskins for making luxury fur coats and accessories. Technically, the hunters are to sell only skins from seals hunted for food. The skins are salted and sent to the Great Greenland tannery at Qaqortoq, where they are prepared for export. Authorities realize that hunters sometimes violate the restriction against hunting only for the pelts, but they are also aware that without such bending of the rules, many small villages would not be able to survive for long.

FARMING AND HERDING

Families with arable land use it to grow a few table vegetables for home use, including potatoes, tomatoes, carrots, and herbs. In addition, a few hardy grasses and hay grow in the ice-free areas. The grasses and hay provide enough fodder for cattle and sheep. Sheep also feed on spring blossoms and berries, giving Greenland's domestic lamb an unusually fragrant flare. There are also a few reindeer farms, on which the animals are raised for their meat and fur.

The larger markets in Greenland's towns import foods from Denmark and other European countries. Imported foods are expensive, but they provide important variety to the standard diet of meat and fish.

THE GOVERNMENT AND THE ECONOMY

Greenland's need for basic necessities has made it heavily dependent on Denmark. Nearly 60 percent of Greenland's exports (primarily seafood) are shipped to Denmark. Imports consisting of such items as food, machinery,

A farm in Southern Greenland.

medical supplies, and transportation equipment come from Denmark (83 percent), with smaller amounts from Norway and Sweden.

Greenland's government is also involved in the economy through Home Rule. The Home Rule Government is the island's largest employer, with more than 8,000 people working with government contracts. These include such positions as building inspectors, teachers and school administrators, warehouse workers, and media specialists.

The Home Rule Government is also responsible for land distribution. Private ownership of land is not permitted. A person or business wishing to start a company that requires land must request a permit from the government to lease the property for a certain period of time. There are now dozens of small shops operating on leased properties, including electrical repair businesses, restaurants, and retail stores.

A cargo ship moving containers to the port. About 83 percent of Greenland's imports are basic necessities which they obtain from Denmark.

MINERALS

Greenland has some potential for mineral development, but a good deal of time and investment will be needed to develop those resources. The oldest mineral industry was the mining of cryolite, which is also known as Greenland spar. It is a mineral used in the making of aluminum. Once found in only a few places in the world, it is now mined in several locations, with a major mine at Ivittuut in south Greenland and a smaller one at Arsuk.

Oil has been discovered near Jameson Land in eastern Greenland and also on the island's west coast. Valuable deposits of gold, diamonds, tantalite, uranium, and iron have been found, but few of these have been mined. Some coal, marble, zinc, lead, and silver have been mined, but so far only in modest amounts. A good deal of time, effort, and money will be needed to determine the amount and value of these resources.

An aerial view of Disco Harbor, which is being opened up for oil and gas exploration.

ENVIRONMENT

FROM THE AIR THE 1,600-MILE (2,575-km) stretch of the island of Greenland looks like an unspoiled wilderness of snow, ice, rock, and tiny barren islands. But Greenland is troubled by a variety of environmental problems that the Greenlanders themselves did little to create.

For example, centuries of overhunting and overfishing by people throughout the world have decimated many species of fish, whales, and seals. This has led to the setting of strict limits on the harvesting of endangered species. Greenlanders suffer from such restrictions, even though they make very limited catches of key sea mammals, especially whales and seals.

In addition, chemical pollutants produced by modern industries tend to become concentrated at the higher end of the food chain, including the whales and polar bears that the Inuit depend on for food.

In other words, no matter how remote Greenland seems from the rest of the world, its environmental health is intimately tied to events and trends in every other part of the planet. Events in Greenland are clear proof of the interdependence of all parts of Earth.

GLOBAL WARMING

One great fear about global warming is its potential impact on the melting of Greenland's ice cap. The ice cap, the second largest in the world, covers 668,000 square miles (1,730,000 sq km). It is 2 miles (3.2 km) thick and covers an area the size of Mexico. If the entire ice cap melted, it would raise world sea levels by as much as 20 feet (6 m), creating disastrous flooding in coastal regions throughout the world.

Global warming has been the subject of debate for many years. Some scientists and many leaders of government and business have felt that climate warming, if it really is taking place, is probably the result of natural

Opposite: **The ice cap is an important aspect of Greenland's environment. Greenlanders are worried about the impact of the melting ice cap on their country.**

A GLOBAL WARMING SHOCK

Late in December 2006 scientists made a stunning announcement: The Ayles Ice Shelf (*circled in red below*), a huge 41-square-mile (106-sq-km) hunk of ice, had broken loose from the coast of Canada's Ellesmere Island and had already drifted some 40 miles (64 km) out to sea. This new ice island was leaving behind a wake of icy boulders.

Scientists were shocked by the size and suddenness of the event. They quickly concluded that the break had been caused by global warming. They had always assumed that the warmer climate would lead to a slow melting of the ice cap and glaciers. This sudden, large-scale change was totally unexpected.

One scientist, Warwick F. Vincent, who studies Arctic conditions, was stunned by what he saw: "This is a dramatic and disturbing event," he said in an Associated Press interview in December 2006. "It shows that we are losing remarkable features of the North that have been in place for many thousands of years. We are crossing climate thresholds, and these may signal the onset of accelerated change ahead."

Some scientists say it is the largest event of its kind in Canada in 30 years. In commenting on the role of global warming, Vincent said, "The remaining ice shelves in Canada are 90 percent smaller than when they were first discovered in 1906. We aren't able to connect all of the dots . . . but unusually warm temperatures definitely played a major role."

For many years researchers have noticed that several ice shelves in Canada and Greenland have cracked in half. As temperatures continue to warm, new ice islands form and drift away from the Arctic Sea. This raises a new danger—the ice islands may drift into shipping lanes, creating a hazard to ships.

cycles of warming and cooling. But over the years a steadily growing number of scientists have become convinced that only human action, the creation of industrial and vehicular pollution, can explain the rapid changes in climate throughout the world.

Greenland and other Arctic regions have provided important research areas for the world's scientists. These areas are considered Earth's early-warning system because their ecosystems are very sensitive. Serious scientific research has been conducted for more than a century on Greenland, since the first International Polar Year, in 1882–1883. Since then, teams of scientists have tried to understand how clues from the Arctic provide information about life in other parts of the world. Since the 1990s the formation of organizations in the Arctic Council and the International Arctic Science Committee have created unprecedented international cooperation.

THE INTERNATIONAL POLAR YEAR

The International Polar Year (IPY) was instituted in 1882–1883 by European scientists and government leaders. The purpose was to study both the Arctic and Antarctic polar regions. The IPY actually covers two-year periods. The current one is the fourth IPY, from March 2007 to 2009.

Researchers from 130 nations are analyzing global warming and its possible impact on humans and wildlife. The questions being explored include: Is Greenland's ice cap really melting, or is the ice thickness on the east coast increasing enough to offset the decline? If the ice cap melts completely, how much will it raise sea levels around the world? Is it possible that farming will again become possible as it was in the time of the Vikings?

Several researchers have taken core samples from deep in Greenland's ice cap. One study retrieved ice that was frozen roughly 120,000 years ago. The core samples reveal information about climate change over the 120,000-year period.

The unprecedented global cooperation made possible by the IPY resulted in the February 2007 report released by the UN's Intergovernmental Panel on Climate Change (IPCC). This largest of all environmental studies concluded for the first time that global warming was 90 percent likely to be the result of human activity. The contributors to the report, including about 600 scientists representing some 40 countries, also said the climate is destined to warm for the rest of this century—even if all new pollution is eliminated—because of the huge amounts of carbon we have already released into the air.

THE LOSS OF ICE

Ice loss caused by global warming takes place in two ways: the melting of the ice cap and the increased pace of glaciers breaking off into the sea. In February 2006

THE WEIGHT OF THE GREENLAND ICE CAP

The weight of Greenland's ice cap is so great that it has pushed the island's bedrock below sea level, leaving much of the bedrock concealed. Only recently have scientists learned enough to speculate that Greenland might be three separate islands.

Between 1990 and 2000 the average winter temperature at the Swiss station camp had increased by nearly 7°F.

researchers at NASA's Jet Propulsion Laboratory (JPL) and the University of Kansas reported that Greenland's glaciers are melting twice as fast as they were five years ago. By 2005 Greenland was losing ice at a greater rate than anyone expected—an annual loss of 52 cubic miles (217 cu km) per year, according to a recent report by the JPL. Half of the loss was attributed to greater summer melting: the rest was caused by the increased speed of glaciers breaking off and drifting into the sea.

Additional satellite data show that Greenland's largest outlet glaciers have started moving faster. The Kangerlussuaq and Jakobshavn glaciers have doubled their pace. In the west the Helheim Glacier appears to be moving about half a football field's distance every day. The speeded-up flow of the glaciers has caused a dramatic increase in seismic activity. Researchers at Harvard and Columbia universities report that glaciers now generate clusters of earthquakes up to a magnitude of 5.0 on the Richter scale.

So far Greenland's ice loss has contributed less than 1 inch (2.5 cm) per year to the rise in sea levels. At that rate, it would take thousands of years for the ice sheet to melt. But scientists are concerned that the observed acceleration in the rate of melting will lead to rapid climate change in the near future.

THE SPEED OF GLACIAL MELTING

Recent studies indicate that the melting of Greenland's glaciers is occurring at more than twice the speed recorded before the year 2000. The glaciers currently pour more than 1 cubic mile of water into the oceans every week. That is about five times the amount of water the city of Los Angeles uses every year.

TODAY'S NORTHWEST PASSAGE

For several centuries courageous explorers searched for a Northwest Passage—a water route through or around the North American continent. Such a sea route would dramatically shorten the trip by boat from Europe to Asia. Dozens of ships were sunk or locked in the ice in these efforts, and thousands of lives were lost. The elusive passage was never found.

Global warming finally created what those explorers could not find. By 2007 Arctic ice no longer blocked the area above the North American continent, and ships could easily sail between the Atlantic and Pacific oceans. Another result of the melting ice was that several nations, including the United States and Denmark, could now claim ownership of the seabed as part of their territorial waters. Many environmentalists fear that there will be a race to exploit the mineral wealth on the floor of the Arctic Ocean. This could include huge deposits of oil and natural gas, which might extend our dependence on fossil fuels indefinitely. Many Greenlanders worry that there are likely to be oil spills or drilling accidents that would be devastating to the island's environment.

CHEMICAL POLLUTION

Although the Arctic wilderness continues to seem like an image of purity, it has become highly polluted with chemicals—the same pollutants that plague the world's cities. Those pollutants drift over Greenland, which lies in the path of winds blowing over both European and North American cities. Long, dark winters and severe cold inhibit the breakdown of those chemicals, so they build up in the food chain.

As a result, both polar bears and humans have heavy concentrations of pollutants, including PCBs, chemicals dangerous to animals, in their bodies. Nearly all Greenland Inuit have high levels of PCBs and mercury in their systems. A 2003 report by the Arctic Monitoring and Assessment Programme found that mercury levels in Inuit villagers were 20 to 50 times higher than those in urban populations in the United States and Europe.

INTERNATIONAL COOPERATION

Since the first International Polar Year, in 1882–1883, international cooperation in Arctic research has grown steadily. The Second International Polar Year, in the 1930s, brought together researchers from 40 nations, and the third year, also known as the International Geophysical Year, involved a total of 67 nations. The Fourth International Polar Year, involving an estimated 130 nations, will take place in 2007–2008.

One of the many projects being carried out in this fourth cooperative effort is the Arctic Coring Expedition. A series of ocean-drilling projects will produce climate records covering about 50 million years.

THE PLUTONIUM SCARE

Environmental issues have occasionally caused rifts between Greenlanders and the governments of Denmark and the United States. At times actions by either government seem to have disregarded the needs of the islanders, including the need to protect the environment.

A heated issue has involved the American air base at Thule. In January 1968 a B-52 bomber crashed near the base. An ambitious two-month clean up operation followed. Of the 1,000 workers employed in the cleanup, more than 100 died over the next few years, half of them from cancer. A lawsuit was filed by 166 workers in 1968 to find out what was causing the illnesses. Not until 1995 was it made public that the plane had been carrying four nuclear bombs armed with 13 pounds (6 kg) of plutonium. In the meantime the Danish government paid $9,000 tax-free to each of the 1,500 Greenlandic and Danish workers and residents of the base area.

Another surprise was announced in August 2000: Only three of the nuclear bombs had been recovered, meaning that the fourth was still in Greenland. Somewhere between 17 ounces (482 g) and 3 pounds (1.4 kg) of plutonium were never recovered. Both the Americans and Danes have conducted several environmental impact studies, but the results remain secret. Meanwhile, hunters report finding musk oxen, seals, and other animals with birth defects that might have been caused by radiation damage.

The fear of more health problems and anger over the forced relocation of several villages has led many Greenlanders to demand that the base be closed. Instead, its lease was renewed in 2004, and the United States announced plans for expanding it as part of the "Star Wars" missile defense system. The people of Quaanaaq took their plea to move their village back to its traditional location to the Supreme Court in Denmark, but they lost the case. The case has since been moved to the European Court of Human Rights.

ENDANGERED SPECIES

Many Arctic species have been endangered for years, largely as a result of overhunting by people from many countries. This is particularly true of the magnificent whales that once plied the Arctic waters. The northern right whale was brought to the edge of extinction. (It was called the "right" whale because it seemed the ideal species to hunt: it was big, slow-moving, and loaded with blubber to fuel lamps.) It is now one of the rarest of all whales.

Other threatened whales include the bowhead whale, known to live for up to 200 years. Beluga whales are also in danger, and orca, found mostly in Alaska, have declined seriously since the *Exxon Valdez* oil spill in 1989. There are some bright notes. For example, the blue whale, after 40 years of protection, has reappeared in Arctic waters.

Because indigenous people depend on the sparse plant and animal life of the Arctic, they are the first to notice the harmful effects of pollutants and global warming. The people of Greenland took an important step when they established Northeast Greenland National Park in the most

Beluga whales are now on the endangered species list.

remote section of the island. The park is the largest in the world and covers about one-quarter of the island. Because it is isolated from the settled parts of Greenland, it is less likely that the wildlife will be disturbed by humans. The park's tundra, ice cap, and rocky hills provide homes for plenty of musk oxen, polar bears, caribou, Arctic wolves, foxes, seals, and walruses.

The arctic wolf is one of many animals that live in the Northeast Greenland National Park.

GREENLANDERS

DESPITE ITS STATUS AS THE WORLD'S largest island, Greenland has remarkably few people. Fewer than 60,000 live in scattered towns and villages along the coasts. (That many people would be an average crowd at an American baseball game.) About 88 percent of the population was born in Greenland; most of the rest were born in Denmark. Only a small percentage of Greenlanders are full-blooded Inuit. The vast majority have some Danish blood.

Roughly one out of every four Greenlanders lives in the capital, Nuuk. Most of the other 75 percent live in one of the 17 municipalities, and about 10,000 live in 65 small villages, most with fewer than 100 people.

Opposite: **A traditionally dressed Inuit girl.**

Below: **Most Greenlanders live in villages like this.**

MIGRATIONS

Like the American Indians of North America, Greenland's Inuit trace their origins to eastern Asia (Siberia). They were probably the last of the people who migrated over the land bridge that connected Asia and North America across the Bering Strait during the last Ice Age. When the huge glaciers of the Ice Age began to melt about 10,000 years ago, the seas rose, and the land bridge disappeared. Historians believe that the last groups of Inuit migrated across Alaska and Canada on foot, and across the Arctic Sea in small boats.

Although the Norse lived in Greenland for about 400 years, they seem not to have mixed with the Inuit peoples. Not long after the last of the Norse settlers mysteriously disappeared in the late 15th century, other Europeans began to arrive, leading to a good deal of mixing of Inuits and Europeans.

THE POLAR INUIT

From the 16th and 17th century on the Danish influence on the Inuit increased steadily. In the north of the island, however, one group remained isolated. Not only did these people have no contact with Europeans, they also seem to have had little if any communication with the Inuit of southern Greenland.

This group became known as the Inughuit, also known as the Polar Inuit, or the Polar Eskimos. In the 1850s they were joined by a small group of about 60 Inuit who had migrated from Canada. The newcomers reintroduced both bows and arrows and kayaks to the Inughuit.

The Inughuit continued to live in isolation from the rest of Greenland. They still represent the purest of the Inuit today, with little or no mixing with European blood. Only after the mid-1800s was there some mixing of these people and Europeans.

The way of life of the Inughuit is considered to be closest to the traditional way of life of the Inuit before the arrival of Europeans. The Inughuit are great hunters. In their kayaks and the larger, multiperson umiaks, they glide among the ice floes in search of seals, walruses, and polar bears. Several boats, some holding women, together can even take on a whale. A hunter in each boat harpoons the animal. A whale might drag the boats for several miles before it tires and the hunters can finish it off with spears.

A whale is a prized catch. It can provide enough meat to feed several small villages for several weeks. The blubber is also of great value. It is

An Inuit hunter fashions a kayak harpoon.

loaded with vitamin C, one of the essential nutrients that has provided the Inuit with remarkably good health. The blubber also gives them oil for lamps, for heat, and for cooking. The skin, bones, and ivory of many of the animals they hunt are used to make tools, weapons, clothing, and carvings. Today, most Inughuit continue to rely on kayaks, harpoons, and spears for hunting; they look with disdain at the people from the south and from Europe who come north to hunt with rifles and motorized boats.

Another unique feature of life in the north is that the major form of transportation is still the dogsled. There are more than 30,000 sled dogs in Greenland, and they are all purebred. In fact, to avoid crossbreeding, no sled dogs are allowed south of the Arctic Circle, and owners of dogs of other breeds are not allowed to keep them north of the Artic Circle. Consequently, there is no dogsledding around Nuuk or other southern towns.

For centuries Inughuit women made clothing—parkas made of sealskin and boots with fur on the inside. The skin layer is waterproof, while the fur lining provides warmth. Many northern villagers continue to make clothing in the traditional way, but increasingly the Inughuit are following the other Inuit in buying ready-made clothes from retail stores in the larger towns.

THE MIXING OF CULTURES

The mixing of people and influences from the outside world in the past century has been transforming Greenland into a modern society, mixing the old and the new.

In the past the Inuit lived remarkably healthy lives. They hunted sea mammals and land animals, including caribou, musk oxen, and smaller animals, such as arctic hare and fox. Birds also provided an important food source. In the north the Inughuit hunted birds that roosted by the millions on rugged cliffs; in the warm months they lived in tents close to the nesting sites. Geese, ducks, and a variety of seabirds provided variety in the diet and also offered a supply of feathers and down for making clothing. The rich diet, supplemented by berries and other plants available during the brief growing season, seemed to supply all the nutrients they needed.

When the Danes took over the island, they introduced new foods and ways of living that changed those traditional patterns. Not all of the changes were improvements. Two of the most harmful new products introduced were tobacco and alcohol. Many Inuit became addicted to tobacco, and today lung cancer is a major health issue. The abuse of alcohol has also become a serious problem.

Inuit wearing sealskin clothing in Nanortalik.

Over the past 60 or 70 years the Danish government has introduced many changes to the Inuit. New styles of housing were introduced, for example. Huts built of turf and sod were replaced by modern apartment buildings. At first these were alienating to the Inuit, but gradually many adjusted. Others found a compromise: they built single-family wood frame houses, which they painted in bright colors.

The Inuit were urged to take jobs in the new fish-processing plants and to rely less on hunting for their livelihood. But people who had hunted and fished all their lives often had trouble adjusting to living in towns and working in plants. They missed the old days, when they left their houses unlocked, with a pot of coffee on the burner, in case friends dropped in while they were out.

The transition to modern life left some Greenlanders feeling confused, and some spoke of a vague feeling of loss. Much of what they had

The Inuit adapted the new style of housing to suit their own tastes by building single-family wood frame houses and painting them in bright colors.

enjoyed was gone, including a closeness to nature. Many tried to escape with the help of alcohol or drugs. However, a growing number became more clearly focused on building a better future. The 1979 law that established the Home Rule Government has helped give Greenlanders a sense of being able to control their own destiny.

By the 21st century most Greenlanders had made satisfactory adjustments to modern life. Men might hunt seals or caribou using modern weapons and equipment. Except for the Inughuit, most no longer use the traditional kayaks, bows and arrows, and harpoons, but they have not forgotten where and when to hunt or fish. After hunting with modern weapons, they then return home to watch television, play computer games, or engage in a traditional craft, such as carving stone figurines. The children go to school, play soccer or basketball, and complete their homework assignments.

Inuit fishermen load whale meat from their truck to their fish store. The transition from traditional life to a modern one has been difficult for the Inuit.

LIFESTYLE

FOR THE PAST 60 OR 70 YEARS Greenlanders have been living in transition, seeking a balance between their traditions and new ways of living introduced by the Danes, by other Europeans, and by Americans.

While other emerging societies often become urbanized rapidly, this has not happened in Greenland. In fact, the term city cannot really be applied to any community on the island. The island's largest settlements are known by the Danish word by, meaning "town"; smaller villages are called *bygd* (settlement).

LIFE IN NUUK

Nuuk is the capital of Greenland and by far its most populous town, with 16,200 people, including two neighboring villages that can be considered suburbs. The town is located in a picturesque setting, with a backdrop

Left: **The capital of Greenland, Nuuk.**

Opposite: **Greenlanders enjoying an afternoon in the sun.**

Family can be considered as the cornerstone of Greenland's society.

of mountains and dramatic ice-clogged fjords. Like most of the island's larger towns, Nuuk lies on the protected western side of Greenland and south of the Arctic Circle.

There were only ten or twelve families living there when the famous missionary Hans Egede arrived in 1721 and established a trading post. Later hailed as the "Apostle of Greenland," he introduced sweeping social changes, such as an insistence on nuclear families rather than the traditional communal families. Some objected to the new rules and moved away from the town. Later, a severe smallpox epidemic decimated the town's population.

Nuuk managed to survive these tragedies, and during World War II (1939–1945) it served as the administrative center of the island. In the 1950s the Danish government instituted new reforms designed to speed

Greenland into the modern world. Among the changes was the building of large housing blocks. These were more solid and comfortable than traditional housing, but people found them alienating because they did away with the sense of community prevalent in the old neighborhoods.

In addition, government officials felt that providing schools and community services for numerous small villages was inefficient. Many of the small villages were shut down, and the people were moved to Nuuk or other large towns. The number of small settlements was reduced by about half. Many people disliked the changes. They petitioned the government to change the housing patterns back to something more similar to traditional neighborhoods.

After the Home Rule Government was established in 1979, new forms of housing were created. Single-family homes were built out of imported

Many Greenlanders felt a sense of loss of community after the government's relocation program.

wood. The structures, which all look about the same, are usually owned by the government and leased to families. The houses are built into small, rugged hillsides, giving them a sturdy foundation and protection from the wind. People paint their houses in bright colors, making each settlement a picture of colorful hues. Many of the large apartment buildings built in the 1950s are still in use.

Life in Nuuk is not unlike life in an American suburban town, although there are far fewer motor vehicles than in any American community. The entire island has few roads and only four or five stoplights. Still, people do drive from neighboring villages, which serve as Nuuk's suburbs. Parents might drive their children to school or church functions. People can also drive to one of Nuuk's small shopping malls.

Most transportation in the ice-free water of the south is by boat. In the north, where the harbors freeze, people travel by small aircraft or

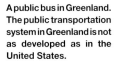

A public bus in Greenland. The public transportation system in Greenland is not as developed as in the United States.

helicopter. There are a few snowmobiles, but they have limited value because of the danger of running out of fuel or tipping over when no help is near.

Most of the workforce is employed in fish-processing plants or in fishing. Great numbers also work for the government as construction workers, teachers, and health clinic workers.

Nuuk and the other large towns have a variety of shopping areas, with grocery stores, meat and fish markets, and specialty stores. Every community of some size has a marketplace called a *Brædtet* where hunters and fishermen can sell their products directly to the public. The displays enable visitors to see the varied selection of meat available, such as musk oxen, lamb, and reindeer; fish, including arctic char, redfish, cod, Greenland halibut, and several varieties of deepwater fish. There are also selections of seal meat and different cuts of whale. Because some of these animals are on the government's list of banned species, agents are likely to confiscate some products.

Nuuk provides a wide variety of activities and places to visit, more than any of the smaller communities. The Katuaq Cultural Center, built in 1997, is a striking architectural achievement; it houses the Greenland Art School and Nordic Institute. The building is used for concerts, lectures, and films and also houses an excellent café. Buildings housing the Home Rule Government and city government are located near the center. The

Most Greenlanders hold jobs in fish-processing plants or in the commercial fishing industry.

Opposite: **The fishing village of Assaqutaq near Sissimiut.**

city also offers an array of outdoor activities, such as hiking, climbing, fishing, kayaking, skiing, and whale watching, as well as indoor swimming pools. There are also a variety of festivals, such as a midsummer marathon that is open to all ages and an arts and music display. In winter many winter sports are available.

VILLAGE LIFE

Greenland's many small villages, usually home to fewer than 100 people, are spread out along the coast in the south and west. There are also a few located on the east coast. All of the villagers follow a combination of a traditional lifestyle and more modern ways of living.

In the northwest corner of Greenland a cluster of villages makes up what is known as the Thule region. The region is almost as large as the nation of Germany, but it is inhabited by fewer than 1,000 people. Three of

NUUK: GREENLAND'S ALMOST CITY

When approaching Nuuk from the north, Greenland's capital is almost completely hidden by Mount Sermitsiaq—a jagged rock formation that features picturesque waterfalls during the summer months. The Atlantic current that flows past the town, and actually surrounds it on three sides, is warm enough to keep the harbor from freezing. The open water enables people to rely on boats for much of their transportation needs.

In addition to being the site of Greenland's Home Rule Government offices, Nuuk is also the island's cultural capital. Major festivals are held there, and it is home to Greenland University and the National Museum and Archives. One of the newest and most striking buildings is Katuaq Cultural Center, which was dedicated in 1997. The wave-shaped building made of wood and glass houses the Greenland Art School, a library, concert hall, cinema, and café. Some of the exhibits on Greenland's history include items returned to the island from Denmark.

the villages in the region—Siorapaluk, Moriasaq, and Qaanaaq—lie closer to the North Pole than to any other communities on Earth. Siorapaluk, a village of about 80 people, is only 730 miles (1,175 km) from the North Pole.

Hunting is the primary means of earning a living in the region, but usually each family needs at least one person to have a salaried job. This income pays for electricity, Internet access, and other items.

The diet of the villagers is composed of mostly traditional foods, such as seal, walrus, caribou, and whale. Hunters continue to wear handmade garments of polar bear skin, anoraks made of caribou, and fur-lined boots. Many of the men are highly skilled users of kayaks and harpoons.

Pressure from environmental groups has led to restrictions on the hunting of certain species, especially the polar bear. Hunters say that the restrictions make it increasingly difficult for them to earn a living. A drop in the price of sealskins that began in the 1980s has also cut into the rural village lifestyle. Most hunters process skins only for their own use, since there is so little profit to be made by selling them.

The warming climate has also impacted the hunters. There is less sea ice. The ice also

Huskies are used to pull sleds. Dogsleds are a common mode of transportation, especially when ice and snow make traveling by motor vehicle impractical.

forms later than it did in the past, and it melts sooner. This shortens the hunting season.

As in the larger communities, the government provides housing for a modest rent. All the homes have modern facilities, although there are no flush toilets. Government workers remove garbage and empty toilets several times a week.

In every village sled dogs outnumber humans. The wolflike huskies are not kept as pets, so they are normally not friendly toward people. As soon as puppies reach the age of six months, they are chained.

Qaanaaq, the largest settlement in the Thule region, has three stores. One store sells clothing, shoes, books, magazines, and newspapers. A second store specializes in hardware, electronics, and equipment for hunting and dogsledding. The third store is a small supermarket. It offers fresh fruit, eggs, cheese, and other fresh foods. Since the produce is flown in by helicopter, the prices are very high. Local products, primarily meat and fish, are sold frozen. Baked goods are sold "right from the oven" every day.

With the help of these stores, the villagers have access to many imported products common in the rest of the world. Children, in particular, have made junk foods a favorite. Soft drinks, chips, and candy bars have raised the incidence of health problems, including obesity. The use of alcohol has also risen at an alarming rate. Less risky in terms of health has been the sudden popularity of the Internet, mobile phones, and video games.

EDUCATION

School is compulsory and free for nine years. Students are taught in the Greenlandic language. Secondary schools are geared toward preparing students to work in the trades, including construction, metalwork, food preparation, animal husbandry, fishing gear manufacture, and technical lab work.

An elementary school teacher with her student. Eduction is both compulsory and free.

A special folk school is located in Sisimiut that is geared toward preserving and teaching Inuit culture. Named the Knud Rasmussen College, it was opened in 1962 with the goal of strengthening students' understanding of their culture.

There are also general-education high schools located in Nuuk, Qaqortoq, Aasiaat, and Sisimiut. Their goal is to keep high school graduates in Greenland to receive their higher education. The University of Greenland is located in Nuuk. As of 2007 it had a staff of 25 and about 100 students. Subjects taught include public administration, cultural and social history, and Greenlandic language and literature. The university is also a member of the University of the Arctic, which has institutions in Lapland, Alaska, and Norway. The curriculum includes circumpolar studies.

Greenland also has a seminary that offers a four-year program to train social workers and primary school teachers.

TRANSPORTATION

Transportation in Greenland is unique. There are no railroads. There are no inland waterways and very few roads between towns. In fact, there are only about 100 miles (161 km) of roads on the entire island. Greenland has no established road system, and domestic travel is performed by foot, boat, or aircraft.

Traditionally, transportation has been by boat along the coast, particularly in the south and west, where the harbors usually remain ice free throughout the year. In the north dogsleds are dominant. People there also have to travel by small plane or helicopter.

Greenland has an unusually good system of air travel. During World War II American forces built several landing fields and airports.

The largest of these, called Bluie West Eight, has now been enlarged, modernized, and renamed Kangerlussuaq Airport. It is the main airport for travel to Greenland and the only one with runways large enough to handle jumbo jets. Greenland now has a total of 18 airstrips, 14 of them paved. While nearly all international flights are handled by Air Greenland, Icelandair operates "day trips to the wilderness," which are excursions from Reykjavik to the east coast of Greenland for a day of hunting, dogsledding, or other sports.

Kangerlussuaq Airport in Greenland.

RELIGION

RELIGION IN GREENLAND HAS GONE through several different phases. Attempts to establish Christianity were frequently unsuccessful until quite recently. In earlier centuries both Catholicism and Protestantism failed to take root among the Inuit.

Over the centuries the traditional Inuit religion has sustained the people and has not changed a great deal. The Inuit follow a complicated form of nature worship. It is based on the belief that everything has a soul, the inue. From that came the word Inuit.

Central to Inuit beliefs is the importance of the shaman. Shamans are similar to priests in other religions, but they are endowed with supernatural powers. In fact, the Greenland Inuit call themselves Kalaaleq, meaning "people with strong shamans."

THE CATHOLIC PERIOD

When the Norse first settled on Greenland in the 10th century, the colonists believed in a pantheon of Norse gods. Christianity was introduced within a few years by Leif the Lucky, the son of Erik the Red. Norse missionaries arrived to help with the conversions and to establish an organized Catholic church. The Norse were quick to adopt Catholicism, and it flourished from about 1000 to 1450.

Above: **Zion church in Ilulissat.**

Opposite: **An altar in a Catholic church in Greenland.**

The Catholic Norse established 16 parishes, along with churches and even a few monasteries. Every settlement soon had a small but sturdy stone church. In some settlements every well-to-do family had its own small church. Many of the ruins still stand today, providing one of the island's fascinating tourist attractions.

When the Norse communities mysteriously vanished, between the late 1300s and about 1450, the official church quickly vanished as well. Over

DANISH LUTHERANISM AND HANS EGEDE

In 1536 Denmark officially became a Lutheran nation. They were called Evangelical Lutherans because they were committed to bringing their faith to others. The official name of the church in Greenland is the Danish National Evangelical Lutheran Church. In 1979 Greenland became an independent Home Rule territory, administered by its own diocese and bishop.

Hans Egede (1686–1758) was the Lutheran missionary who tried to convert the Inuit, but he encountered a lot of bad luck. Some in his party brought smallpox to the island. Many were stricken by the deadly disease, including his wife.

After his wife's death, Egede planned to return to Denmark. But first he tried to persuade the Inuit to give up living in communal or group families in favor of nuclear families made of husband, wife, and children. Few Inuit welcomed the change, and it led to deep splits in some groups; some leaders encouraged their followers to set up new villages.

After Egede moved back to Denmark, he left his sons to carry on his work. The community in which Egede lived, Godthaab, managed to survive and prosper. During World War II it served as Greenland's administrative center, usually called Nuuk at that point. Evangelical Lutheranism remains the island's main religion and Hans Egede continues to be revered as the Apostle of Greenland.

the next two or three hundred years some explorers and missionaries remained convinced that a few Catholics would have survived, perhaps living among the Inuit. But no survivors were ever found, and there was no sign that any Inuit groups had been converted.

LATER CHRISTIANIZING EFFORTS

Nearly 300 years after the disappearance of the Norse, Christianity returned to Greenland with the arrival of the Danish missionary Hans Egede, in

A service being conducted in one of Greenland's churches. Christianity was reintroduced to Greenland by Hans Egede.

1721. He managed to convert a few Inuit to the Lutheran religion. Other missionaries came and struggled to Christianize the people they called "the savage Eskimos." After a century of dedicated effort there were four mission stations, and by the mid-1800s there were more than 1,500 Lutherans, about 900 adults, and 700 children.

TRADITIONAL INUIT RELIGION

Although Evangelical Lutheranism is the official religion, traditional Inuit beliefs continue to have a strong influence on people's lives. In the north, where many communities continue to live by hunting, people also live by the religious traditions of their ancestors.

The Inuit religion is based on the premise that everything has a soul, including rocks, clouds, and other inanimate objects. Humans are believed to have several souls, with the souls of the left side of the torso and the larynx being the strongest. Illness is caused when one or more souls have left the body and have to be brought back from this "small death."

The task of the shaman was to restore the balance between good and evil. It is believed that shamans have special skills that empower them, while in a trance, to enter the spirit world and bring the stricken soul back to health.

Shamans undergo a long period of training, which includes fasting as a way to free the spirit in order to acquire knowledge. They also acquire skill on the sacred drum. The drum is flat and oval shaped. The drum dance was once said to be the only true Inuit music. For several years the dance was rarely used, but it has experienced a revival in the 21st century as a form of entertainment. Shamans use the steady, pulsing rhythm to help them enter a trance. The trance, in turn, gives them the power to become invisible, to fly, and to visit the dead in order to restore a sick person to health.

In the traditional belief system there are no churches, temples, or other religious structures. There are no sermons, either, and even as the Inuit have adopted many Christian beliefs and practices, the teachings of the Bible have not played a prominent role in Inuit life.

One ancient practice that has remained constant is the use of amulets. These are small carved figures that represent spirits or gods and can help ward off harm or evil. Amulets are particularly important during the hunt. Animals allow themselves to be taken only if a hunter's spirit is in harmony with the spirits of the animals. If that harmony does not exist, the hunt will be a disaster. After a hunt it is important to give thanks to the animals' spirits.

Echoes of traditional beliefs and practices can be seen at community festivals. The first light of spring is the occasion for traditional ceremonies and celebrations. Amulets made of a variety of materials have become favorite craft items.

THE *TUPILAK*

In the late 19th century an explorer named Gustav Holm became fascinated by the spiritual helper of the shamans, called a *tupilak*. Holm asked several shaman what the *tupilaks* were. The shaman were not sure how to respond. They shared some ideas, but when some of them tried to carve samples they came out quite different.

The result was a new Inuit art form. *Tupilaks* are carved out of whale's teeth. The figures are rather grotesque, with twisted grins. Several modern carvers, such as Aron and Cecilie Kleist, have become famous, and their *tupilak* carvings have become museum attractions.

LANGUAGE

Opposite: **A sign written in Greenlandic.**

THE OFFICIAL LANGUAGE IS GREENLANDIC—one of several Inuit dialects spoken in the Arctic regions. There are many variations within the Greenlandic spoken in different parts of the island as well. The two major dialects of the language of Greenland are known as West Greenlandic and East Greenlandic. Variations in West Greenlandic can be understood throughout the West Greenlandic region, but people from the west cannot always understand people from the east.

Although the Inuit language dates back several thousand years, there was no organized, written form of it until about 150 years ago. The first book written in Inuit was penned by the Danish-Norwegian missionary Hans Egede in 1742. It was printed in the Roman alphabet, and Egede used the letter *r* to represent a sound made in the back of the throat. A century later, in 1851, the written form of the language was systematized by Samuel Kleinschmidt, a German orthographer. He introduced accents to differentiate long sounds from short ones and made other improvements. Kleinschmidt's work transformed Egede's model into a useful system of writing.

SAMPLE WORDS AND PHRASES

Hello	*Inuugujoq*
Good-bye, best wishes.	*Inuulluari.*
Bye, see you soon.	*Inuullaritse.*
Yes	*Aap*
No	*Naagga/Naamik*
Thank you (very much).	*Qujanaq.*
What's your name?	*Qanoq ateqarpit?*
My name is . . .	*Imik ateqarpunga . . .*

When the Danish government took control of Greenland, the Danish language was taught in schools. Many students now learn Danish as well as Greenlandic, and the literacy rate was reported to be 93 percent in 2005. While the vast majority of Greenlanders speak Greenlandic, many can also speak Danish, and a few speak English.

LANGUAGE WITHOUT WORDS

Greenlanders have a relaxed concept of time. They are not "clock watchers" and seem to accept delays without complaint. When Greenlanders

NUMBERS

Numbers in Greenlandic only go from 1 to 12. After 12, all numbers are referred to as *amerlasoorppassuit* (meaning "many"), although some use Danish numbers, starting with 10.

Number	Greenlandic
1	*ataaseq*
2	*marluk*
3	*pingasut*
4	*sisamat*
5	*tallimat*
6	*arfinillit*
7	*arfineq marluk*
8	*arfineq pingasut*
9	*qulingiluat*
10	*quilit*
11	*arqanillit*
12	*arqaneq marluk*

are late for meetings, foreign visitors sometimes assume this is due to carelessness.

In general, Greenlanders do not engage in conversation easily. Europeans often interpret this as signs of shyness or even rudeness. Greenlanders can also cause misunderstanding because they love to laugh and chuckle; to Europeans or Americans these outbursts sometimes seem out of place or excessive.

SPEAKING GREENLANDIC

The pronunciation of both vowels and consonants is difficult. Consonants come from deep in the throat, and some vowels are hardly pronounced at all.

VOWELS

a	as the '*u*' in 'hut'
aa	as the long '*a*' in 'father'
e	as the '*a*' in 'ago'
i	as in 'marine'
o	as in 'hot'
u	as the '*oo*' in 'cool'

CONSONANTS

Consonants are pronounced as they are in English, with these exceptions:

g	as in 'goose'
j	as in 'jaw'
k	as in 'key'
l	as in 'leg'
ng	as in 'sing'
q	pronounced as a '*k*' from deep in the back of the throat
v	as in 'van'

Other Greenlandic cultural traits that simply require awareness on the part of foreigners include raising eyebrows to mean yes and squinting to signify no, with no words being spoken. A visitor who does not understand this language without words can face a difficult time.

THREE-LANGUAGE LISTS

In Greenland's major towns, the large supermarkets frequently list items in three languages—Greenlandic, Danish, and English. Here are a few samples.

Greenlandic	Danish	English
aalisakkaq	*fisk*	fish
aarrup negaa	*hvalrusked*	walrus meat
arferup negaa	*hvalked*	whale meat
egaluk pujogag	*saelked*	seal meat
nilaap ernga	*isvand*	ice water

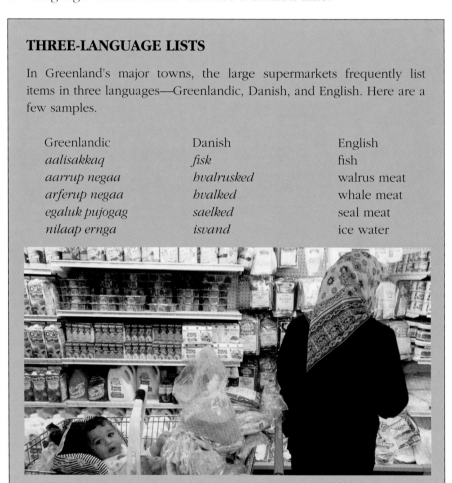

NAME CHANGES

When Greenland was granted Home Rule in the 1970s, many place names were changed from Danish to Greenlandic. Technically, the correct name for Greenland is Kalaallit Nunaat. The name of the capital became Nuuk, replacing Godthaab. And technically, the correct name for the West Greenlandic language is Kalaallisut.

Some Greenlandic names express the major features of a place. Lichtenau, for example, was changed to Alluitsoq, meaning "a place with few breathing holes for seals"; Julianehaab became Qaqortoq (*below*), which means "a white place"; and Frederikshaab became Paamiut, or "place at the mouth of the fjords."

ARTS

IN SPITE OF ITS SMALL AND scattered population, Greenland has a remarkably active arts community. Their work ranges from ancient crafts that have been created for centuries to experimental and avant-garde works that are admired throughout the world. Every large town has a museum displaying local artists' work; government offices, including the postal service and tourist offices, also make the work of local artists accessible.

Opposite: **The Stone and Man sculpture project was initiated by Greenlander artist, Aka Høegh, in the town of Qaqortoq from 1993–94.**

Below: **Carvings out of whale teeth called *tupilak*.**

The island itself offers a great variety of inspirational themes for artists, such as the dazzling displays of light, including the shows of the aurora borealis and the misty and mysterious vastness of the great ice caps. In addition, picturesque harbors, dramatic fjords, and quaint villages with

brightly colored houses add to the variety of landscapes. As the artist Aage Gitz-Johansen has said, "It's hard not to be inspired," and maybe that is why Greenland displays such a remarkably rich artistic life.

TRADITIONAL ARTS AND CRAFTS

A local craftsman carves narwhal bone into jewelry.

Carving is the oldest and best known of Greenland's traditional art forms and dates back many centuries. Simple household tools and utensils were

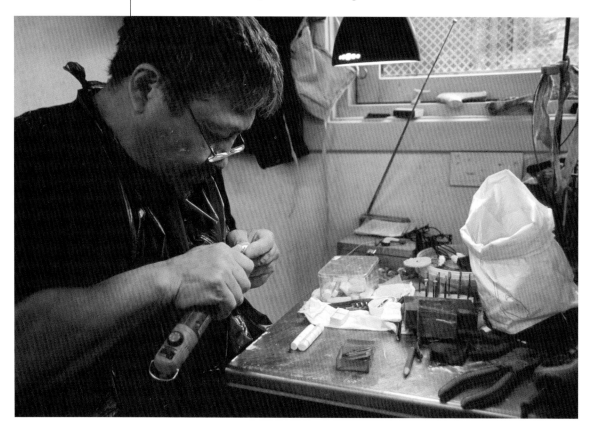

carved out of natural materials, such as driftwood, bone, and soapstone. The sculptures soon branched out into carvings of animal models, jewelry, and strange-looking figurines known as *tupilak*.

Tupilak were originally figurines that shamans used to cast spells over enemies. By the 20th century *tupilak* were transformed into artistic creations without spiritual significance. Such famous contemporary artists as Aron and Cecilie Kleist produce *tupilak* figures that are on display in museums and galleries.

Sculptors today use a variety of natural materials, including soapstone, antlers, narwhal tusks, bones, and walrus ivory. An interesting new

THE GREENLAND KAYAK

The kayak, or *qajaq* as it is called in Greenland, was first developed almost 4,000 years ago and has undergone many changes over the years. Earlier the kayak was covered with sealskin from which the hair was removed, but today most are constructed with a nylon or canvas outer skin. In Greenland's hunting districts, such as Qaanaaq, hunters are still required to hunt for narwhals according to tradition, that is, from a traditional *qajaq* with lances and spears thrown by hand.

From an early age boys learn to master the "Greenlandic roll." Dressed in waterproof clothing, they learn how to use the move if the boat tips over. Small oars help them to turn the boat the rest of the way over, bringing the paddler upright again.

Both men and women work on the construction of kayaks. Men gather driftwood for the frame, and women sew the fabric together from three to four skins of the harp seal, which they then stretch over the frame. Modern kayaks and those used for recreation are made of fiberglass, which can better withstand the rough seas.

form of carving has been developed in the town of Qaqortoq. The hills surrounding the town are covered in boulders that a team of sculptors are transforming into exciting sculptures of human and animal forms. This is known as the Stone and Man sculpture project, developed in 1993 by the famed artist Aka Høegh, who led a team of 18 artists in transforming the village into a striking sculpture garden.

Another traditional craft—jewelry making—has been largely the work of women, most of them retired. They work primarily with beads, especially tiny *saparngaq*. The colors are sometimes garish, but the best work is delicate and beautiful.

FROM ORAL TRADITION TO LITERATURE

The tales, chants, and songs of the ancient shaman were believed to have magical powers, so the words and tunes were carefully passed down from generation to generation. This oral tradition has changed very little, but over time many of the pieces were lost. In the 1860s the Danish governor H. J. Rint began to write down the stories and poems. The explorer Knud Rasmussen recorded more, between 1914 and 1924. Rasmussen expanded some of the stories, creating tales with moral lessons, much like Aesop's Fables.

Written language is a recent addition to Greenlandic culture. Writing stories, novels, and plays has become a popular pastime for many people, and the Greenlandic Society of Authors now has about 100 members. Very little Greenlandic literature has been translated into English. One exception is Michael Fortescue's sampler called *From the Writings of the Greenlanders* (1990), which contains stories from the 1920s through the 1980s.

LEADING FIGURES IN THE ARTS

Although born in Denmark, the painter Gitz-Johansen (1897–1977) has long been associated with paintings of the people and landscape of Greenland. He gained fame as a defender of the traditional Greenlandic way of life and also as a critic of the insensitive and fast-paced changes imposed by the Danish government. His work continues to be popular and is on display throughout Scandinavia.

Nanu Disco is a music project that involved the collection of songs from throughout Greenland over the past 80 to 90 years. Performers located throughout the island were recorded live via satellite. Some older performances were re-recorded from records made by travelers. The final product, called *In Search of the Roots*, was written and recorded in less than two months.

Several leading poets, such as Mathias Storch (1883–1957) and Otto Sandgreen (1914–1999), have written powerful poems about the wrenching changes experienced by the Greenlanders from 1945 on.

Laila Hansen is an actress, filmmaker, and promoter. In her film, *Inuk Woman City Blues*, she acts, sings, dances, and presents a tender, loving narration. She is currently raising money to create documentaries on Inuit women.

Born in 1925, Greenland's Jens Rosing has dazzled his countrymen with his versatile creativity—he has excelled in writing and telling stories, painting, and illustrating books. Between 1957 and 2001 he designed more than 150 stamps for the Greenland postal service, earning him the title "The Old Man of Greenland Stamps." In 1980 he was awarded the Danish Authors' Association Prize for Popular Science.

Aron of Kangeq (1825–1869) was a seal hunter who also had remarkable drawing and painting skills. His talents were discovered by a missionary, Samuel Kleinschmith, and then by the Danish natural scientist Dr. Heinrich J. Rink, who spent his spare time collecting folktales. Rink asked Aron to illustrate his collected tales. Aron agreed, although he was bedridden with tuberculosis. His paintings filled a famous four-volume collection called *Legends from Greenland*.

Aka Høegh is widely regarded as Greenland's cultural ambassador. Over several decades she has put on exhibitions that have helped put Greenland's artists on the world map. She is one of the island's first professional artists—that is, earning a living from her art—and the first to gain an international reputation. She was also the instigator of the "Stone and Man" sculpture project in Qaqortoq.

MUSIC AND DANCE

Just as modern Greenlandic literature was built on ancient traditions, modern music and dance have evolved out of the ancient drum dance. The drum dance was an ancient ritual used by shamans for many years. The traditional drum had an oval frame covered with a polar bear's bladder. Over several centuries the drum dance was nearly forgotten but has recently made a comeback and is now considered a precious part of the Greenlanders' heritage. Most efforts to revive the drum dance involve gospel music that uses the drum, gospel songs, and dances originally performed by Dutch and Scottish whalers.

Among young people, rock music has become popular, and several rock groups are producing records that sell. The first Greenlandic rock album, recorded by a group called Sume (meaning "where"), was cut in 1973. In 1976 Greenland's leading record company, named ULO, was founded to support Greenlandic youth music, with a studio in Sisimiut.

Modern Greenlandic music ranges from traditional Inuit drumming to a mix of country and western, polka, reggae, and even bits of traditional Inuit throat singing.

THEATER AND FILM

The Silamiut Theater, established in 1984, is Greenland's only professional theater. The founding members were educated in Denmark. The theater has produced more than 20 plays for children, families, and

Opposite: **An elderly Inuit man plays a traditional flat drum where only its rim is hit.**

Below: **A local choir group performs.**

adults. The members work with a variety of forms—musicals, modern dance, traditional drum dancing, TV, video, and radio productions. In addition, CDs and records have been released, and the company has toured throughout the Scandinavian countries, Europe, North America, and Australia.

Both theater and film have been used to take an unflinching look at the island's social problems. Laila Hansen's *Inuk Woman City Blues* tells the story of Greenlandic women who leave the island looking for a better life in Copenhagen, Denmark's major city. Many of them end up as alcoholics living in poverty. One woman tells how she emerged from 25 years in an alcoholic haze and started a career as a social worker, helping others to recover and often to return to Greenland. The music and poetic narration makes this unlike conventional documentaries.

MUSEUMS AND GALLERIES

There is a museum in just about every town, offering a wide range of art—from ancient to modern. The National Museum in Nuuk is located in

HUMOR WITH A MESSAGE

To mark the 25th anniversary of Home Rule, in 2004, a team of filmmakers made a tongue-in-cheek film for a Danish gallery. They set the scenes in a prison camp and accompanied them with military music. The film told of Greenland's "invasion of the world." The Greenlanders used "ice weapons" to stop global warming. They also used new Inuit names to replace the "impossible-to-pronounce" Danish place names. In spite of the sarcasm, the film encouraged people to think seriously about environmental issues.

the historical region near the colonial harbor. One of the oldest exhibits is the world-famous mummies from Qilakitsoq. Discovered in northern Greenland in 1972, the mummies are extremely well preserved. They date to about 1475 and give a good picture of clothing from that period. Turf dwellings have been preserved near many of the town museums. These have been well cared for and give a striking picture of what homes were like until the 1950s.

There are also theme-oriented buildings, such as the aircraft museums in Kangerlussuaq and Narsarsuaq. These demonstrate the influence of the U.S. air base in the days before, during, and immediately after World War II. There are also picturesque wooden churches located near the museums. The museums in Ilulissat and Nuuk contain the famous nature paintings of Greenland's Emanuel A. Petersen.

The former home of Greenland's hero, Knud Ramussen, is now a museum.

LEISURE

THE SUMMER MONTHS ARE THE most relaxing time in Greenland. Most people live on the western side of the island, where the land is most protected from the fierce Arctic winds.

For several weeks in the summer, the sun does not set. As the snow melts, freshwater streams bubble across the land, and carpets of wildflowers create splashes of color on every hillside.

This is the best time of year for making social visits and shopping. People leave their houses unlocked so that friends can enter. There is always a pot of coffee on the stove or a thermos full of it so visitors can help themselves. Friends may greet each other warmly, then settle in for an hour or two of sitting comfortably in silence, feeling no need to talk. Other social contacts are a good deal livelier.

SHOPPING

Greenlanders have responded with enthusiasm to many of the changes brought about by modernization. People enjoy taking trips to the new malls located on the outskirts of the larger towns. Fruit and vegetable products tend to be expensive because of the transportation costs involved in bringing them to market, but dairy products are inexpensive.

Greenlandic handicrafts are sold in just about all towns. The most common items are objects carved from bone and reindeer antler or from soapstone. Jewelry and *tupilak* are also available, as are worked leather hides and pearls.

A special market known as "The Board" is an open fish and meat market where people can buy whale meat, reindeer, musk ox, seal, fish, and berries (in season). One is located in the port area of almost every town. Greenlanders call these shops Kalaaliaraq, "The Little Greenlander."

Opposite: **Children enjoy an afternoon playing on swings.**

NIGHTLIFE AND ENTERTAINMENT

Most major towns have both pubs and restaurants. Prices there are high, but these places are lively, the place for plenty of drinking, dancing, and noisy sing-alongs. The music usually played in them is hymns. Greenlandic dancing is primarily an adaptation of reels learned from Dutch and Scottish whalers who visited the island in the 18th century.

North of the Arctic Circle and in parts of eastern Greenland, life can be hard during the winter months, when the harsh winter closes in and people feel isolated from their neighbors and from other villages. The Internet has provided an excellent remedy. An Internet café in Nuuk, the capital, connects Greenland with the world. Hundreds of villages and homes have their own computers as well. The Internet provides people with an ideal way to learn more about the world beyond their island, and it puts them in touch with vital medical and educational information.

SPORTS

Few people are more sports-minded than Greenlanders. Not surprisingly, they have a special passion for winter sports. Nearly all of these sports are engaged in during the summer months, since the winter is generally too cold, except for winter endurance contests, such as dogsled races.

The Nuuk Marathon is a classic one that is a more demanding contest than most city marathons. It is run in August over hilly terrain and, although it is still summer, temperatures are often in single digits. The route covers two circuits of a course covering 13 miles (20,922 m). The route contains spectacular scenery—past beautiful old houses from the 1700s, to the harbor, then out of the city, past the airport, to the new district of Qinngorput, with an attractive mountain background and modern Arctic architecture.

Since the first Nuuk Marathon, in 1990, the number of runners has increased steadily to nearly 400 entrants, including many with international credentials. Travel agencies now offer special package deals, making the contest a growing tourist attraction.

Another popular race is undertaken by participants, working in pairs. They take off on a five-day race called the Greenlandic Iron Man, also known as the Greenland Adventure Race. The race alternates between running, cycling, and kayaking (which replaces swimming in the traditional Iron Man competition).

The first stage of 12.5 miles (20 km) takes the competitors over a glacier, then crosses a river. The second stage consists of 31 grueling miles (50 km) of mountain biking. The third stage is the hardest. The run covers 27 miles (43 km) and includes several high-altitude mountain passes. The fourth stage involves kayaking in fjords, and the fifth stage, running, involves about 19 miles (31 km).

In 2002 Nuuk co-hosted the Arctic Games, Olympic-style games for polar competitors. Typical competitions include a variety of balance games, snow-stake throwing, target high kicking with one leg (*aratsiaq*) or with two (*akratcheak*). Another sport, something like arm wrestling, is called finger pulling (*aksaraq*).

The Arctic Circle Race is a cross-country ski race, held annually since 1995, and is one of the world's most grueling Nordic skiing events. From the town of Sisimiut, 40 miles (64 km) north of the Arctic Circle, participants travel 100 miles (161 km) in three days. Rough terrain and late winter storms add to the difficulties. Two nights are spent camping on the tundra with dogsled teams nearby, in case of emergency.

Ice golf is one of Greenland's most unusual sports. Golfers use a larger, somewhat softer ball painted bright yellow. The "greens," of course, are white, and the game provides a variety of unusual hazards, such as cold temperatures, sudden snowstorms, and rugged terrain. The World Ice Golf Championship has drawn golfers from all over the world to the north Greenland course since 1997, while 2007 was the first year for the Lake Ferguson Masters, at Kangerlussuaq in western Greenland.

Most Greenlandic villagers take their soccer seriously, even though the landscape and the climate make it difficult to establish suitable pitches (playing fields). There is so much gravel, for example, that players are reluctant to dive for the ball. Because the distance between settlements makes it impossible to form leagues, annual tournaments are held in late August. No admission is charged, because the pitches are not fenced. The Sports Confederation of Greenland has applied for an exemption from

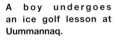

A boy undergoes an ice golf lesson at Uummannaq.

World Cup soccer qualifiers. So far, however, it does not seem likely that Greenland will be allowed to compete in the World Cup because of the lack of facilities.

A variety of other international sports are also popular in Greenland. These include cross-country skiing, indoor soccer, snowboarding, volleyball, snowshoeing, table tennis, and badminton.

Several other competitions are held that are not athletic in nature, such as throat singing, contests in which the singer makes two tones at once. Traditionally, two women stand facing each other, with one challenging the other to repeat the sounds she makes.

Soccer is a popular game with many Greenlanders, especially among the young.

FESTIVALS

GREENLANDERS CELEBRATE A VARIETY of holidays throughout the year. Religious holidays follow the traditional Christian calendar, including Christmas, Easter, and various holy days. Secular holidays include New Year's Day, Constitution Day, and National Day.

One feature of Greenland that influences its festivals is the extreme variation in the length of daylight received. Christmas, for instance, falls during the winter, when the sun rises for very short periods. Greenlanders banish the darkness with lots of Christmas lights. Reddish-orange Christmas stars and numerous candles illuminate the windows of offices and homes from the first Sunday in Advent (four weeks before Christmas) until Twelfth Night (January 6).

At the opposite end of the calendar, National Day is celebrated on June 21, the longest day of the year, when the sun never sets in Greenland. Every town and village celebrates with morning songs, speeches, and flag raising, followed by day-long partying and entertainment.

Opposite: **Inuit children play a game at a party to celebrate the return of the sun.**

CELEBRATING THE RETURN OF THE SUN

After weeks of constant nighttime and star-studded skies, the people of northern Greenland eagerly await the first streaks of light on the horizon. People who live north of the Arctic Circle celebrate with school or family excursions. Some schools take trips to well-known hills, often traveling by dogsled, to welcome the first sunlight with songs, poems, festive foods, and thermoses filled with coffee or hot chocolate.

NATIONAL DAY

National Day is celebrated on June 21, the longest day of the year, when the sun never sets. The holiday was established in 1983 as one of the symbols of Home Rule. The day is called Ullortuneq ("the longest day")

NATIONAL CLOTHING

Traditional Inuit clothing was made of animal skins and hides. People selected the best pelts for warmth and long wear. Both men and women wore furs, trousers, and boots with fur on the inside for extra warmth. The eastern Greenlanders favored a pullover jacket called an anorak, which was usually made of seal or caribou.

When the Europeans came, they brought with them colorful beads and a variety of fabrics, such as sturdy woolens. Glass beads were easy to use, and women began sewing them into fabrics with increasing abundance. The national dress became more and more colorful, with bright hand-knit sweaters, fur or woolen pants, and seal-skin boots with white fur lining. Women displayed their greatest artistry in embroidering the tops.

People wear the Greenlandic national costume with pride on special occasions, including birthdays, weddings, confirmations, and the first day of school. The arrival of a cruise ship is another occasion for wearing the national costume.

and is celebrated in every town and village. The day begins with songs, speeches, the hoisting of the flag, and church services. Entertainment continues throughout the day and includes music, folk dances, displays of such skills as kayaking and crafts, and festive foods.

The day is also celebrated by museums and other cultural centers with special exhibits or events. The national television channel, KNR, airs special programs and reports from different towns throughout the day.

Celebrating National Day is considered an important expression of national unity. The national flag is on display everywhere, many people wear national costumes, and the national anthem is heard often.

RELIGIOUS FESTIVALS AND HOLIDAYS

Greenlandic religious festivals follow the traditional Christian calendar. Christmas is perhaps the most important festival, and it is celebrated from Advent (early December) to early January (Twelfth Night, January 6). The constant glow of candles, Christmas stars, and decorated trees creates a pleasant atmosphere throughout the long holiday. According to a long-standing tradition, decorations stay up until Twelfth Night.

Another tradition occurs on Christmas Eve, when children gather in front of people's homes to sing carols and receive cookies and other treats. Some children receive their presents on the morning of Christmas Eve, others later in the day. In the evening families often dance around the tree and share mulled wine plus a variety of holiday foods.

The New Year is celebrated twice. First there are fireworks and a festive meal eaten at 8:00 P.M. The time corresponds to the New Year in Denmark, where there is a four-hour time difference. The festivities are repeated at midnight Greenland time, including a second round of fireworks and feasting.

Easter is celebrated over several days, from Maundy Thursday through Easter Sunday and Monday. Other religious holidays are observed but without any special festivities. These include Common Prayer's Day, four weeks after Good Friday; Ascension Day, six weeks after Maundy Thursday; and Whitmonday, seven weeks after Easter Monday. Lutheran ministers urge parishioners to observe these holidays, but people are rarely enthusiastic. It is often said that on Sundays and special holidays, churches hold more candles than people.

Greenland is the official home of Santa Claus and all letters addressed to him are put in this huge mailbox.

OTHER SPECIAL EVENTS

In the past the summer period during which people moved inland to hunt and gather wild foods became known as Aasivik, or "Summer Settlement." It was a time for people to meet old friends, share stories and enjoy various forms of entertainment. The custom died out for a time but was revived in 1976 as a two-week social and political event, during which people encouraged traditional theater, drum dances, and folk music. Although the event declined in popularity, a revival in 2006 featured pop music.

Another summer event that has no trouble attracting people is the Aasiaat Rock Festival. Bands come from all over Greenland as well as from Scandinavia, the United Kingdom, and Italy.

The Nuuk Snow Sculpture Festival has been held in February every year since 1994 (with the exception of 2004, when there was not enough snow). Over a four-day period, sculptors from all over the world create fantastic shapes out of huge blocks of compacted snow. Each block measures 10 x 10 x 10 feet (3 x 3 x 3 m). A panel of artists and architects judges the creations and awards prizes.

TWO UNUSUAL EVENTS

Ilulissat celebrates two special events. In April the Arctic Palerfik, a three-day family dogsledding trip along the icefjord, is held. More than 200 people lead about 1,000 dogs through dazzling scenery, with frequent stops to visit with families along the way.

The town also hosts the Arctic Midnight Orienteering Festival in late June or early July. The event consists of several races over four different distances through a rugged and dramatic landscape.

FOOD

FOR MUCH OF THE ISLAND'S HISTORY the Inuit diet consisted almost exclusively of meat and fish. Seal meat was the most common, while whale meat and blubber were also popular. The Inuit also hunted birds, caribou, and musk ox. In addition, they fished for Arctic char, halibut, salmon, and cod. The fish were often dried, smoked, or pressed with herbs, practices that continue today.

A variety of wild foods, which were abundant for short periods in summer and early autumn, supplemented the meat and fish diet. In August and September, for example, blueberry and blackberry bushes were loaded with fruit that provided tasty desserts and salads. Garden angelica is a ball-topped plant that made excellent pickles and jams. Wild thyme was used as a food seasoning and for brewing tea. Arctic harebells were also abundant, and there violet blue blossoms were eaten as a ready-

Left: **Arctic harebells are a part of Greenland's cuisine.**

Opposite: **Local fishermen sell their catch to townspeople through this shop in Sisimiut.**

An orange birch bolete mushroom, which is commonly added to meat dishes.

made salad. A mushroom known as slippery jack or birch bolete was common throughout southern Greenland and made a popular addition to meat dishes.

The diet of mostly meat and fish was a remarkably healthy one for people who required great reserves of energy to combat the fiercely cold weather. Nutritionists' studies indicate that the Inuit had one of the world's lowest rates of cardiovascular disease. The diet was also healthy because the food was organic; no pesticides or fertilizers were involved in the raising of the animals, fish, and wild plants.

THE NEW AND THE OLD

The arrival of the Danes and other Europeans, beginning in the early 1700s, brought some dramatic changes to the Inuit diet. Greenlanders

A hearty breakfast in Greenland. The arrival of the Europeans and Danes influenced the diet and cuisine of Greenlanders.

now eat mutton (lamb), shellfish, potatoes, vegetables, and canned foods. The introduction of alcohol and tobacco has had a devastating effect on the Inuit's health. Both alcoholism and lung disease became serious health issues, and they continue to be Greenland's most serious health problems in the 21st century.

Many of the old ways continue to be part of Greenlandic customs. Although there is now a greater variety of foods available to every home, the traditional meal of meat and fish is still preferred.

Eating customs and values also remain little changed. The traditional hunting way of life established a strong sense of solidarity among the Inuit, for example, and that feeling of unity continues. In the past, when several families worked together to land a whale, they shared in the work of carving the meat and blubber, and they divided everything, including the bones and ivory for crafts. Everything was shared equally, and that sharing was extended to hospitality toward guests.

Mealtimes today reveal the same practice of sharing, no matter how much or how little there is to share. On special occasions, extended

WHALE BLUBBER

Although the idea of eating whale blubber seems pretty unappetizing to most outsiders, it has long been vital to the Greenlandic way of life. It has provided oil for lamps and for cooking. As part of the diet, blubber is packed with vitamins and fat that helps the body hold in heat. Even a thin slice can be chewed on for two or three hours, much as Americans chew gum.

families gather together and enjoy leisurely meals of several courses stretched over an entire day.

GREENLANDIC DINING

Mealtime formalities are few and simple. Family members and guests remove their shoes when they enter a house. Food preparations are also simple; very little seasoning is used, other than salt and pepper. Even though every dish is simple, there is usually enough variety to please everyone's tastes.

One of the favorite dishes is a soup called *suaasat.* It has a meat base, usually seal, whale, or reindeer. Water and rice are added and, as the mixture simmers, cut-up pieces of potato and onion are added. The soup is served as a one-dish meal and usually satisfies everyone. "*Tassa mamaq!*" someone will say. "This tastes great!"

Dried fish or meat are favorite foods for lunch or snacks. Cod, halibut, and whale are all delicious dried and are frequently accompanied by whale blubber. Other dried-food favorites include *ammasat,* made with a small, herringlike fish. Another dish is made with reindeer meat, whale skin, and blubber. This is called *maltak,* and it may be the all-time favorite among Greenlanders. Blackberries and blueberries are eaten with meals or incorporated into cakes and other desserts.

DINING OUT

During the almost endless daylight of summer, Greenlanders like to serve their meals out-of-doors. A favorite picnic meal is freshly caught cod grilled over an open fire and served on a flat stone. The grilled fish is usually served with other fish, meat, and fresh vegetables.

Other favorite outdoor meals include smoked salmon; roast meat with slippery jack mushrooms; blue mussels taken from shallow southern waters (the mussels are steamed or fried and served with butter and garlic); and both snow crabs and shrimp, which are primarily exported but are a great treat when available.

Greenlanders do not dine out in restaurants often, except for business meetings or for special celebrations. Visitors can sample standard Greenlandic foods at outstanding restaurant buffets. In addition, well-known international dishes often make use of Greenlandic ingredients, such as seal or whale meat, whale blubber, and musk ox or reindeer steaks.

GREENLAND HALIBUT STEW

This recipe is a variation on the popular soup called suaasat. Makes 6 servings.

 2 tablespoons olive oil
 1 onion, finely chopped
 1 clove garlic, finely chopped
 fresh parsley, chopped
 2 14-ounce cans stewed or chopped tomatoes
 2 pounds Greenland halibut or cod, chopped into bite-sized chucks
 2 cups 5-minute rice (optional)
 salt and pepper

Heat olive oil in a large iron skillet. Add the onion and sauté. Add the garlic and parsley, and simmer for about 5 minutes. Add the tomatoes, and continue to cook over low heat for 15 minutes. To make a fairly thick stew rather than a soup, add the rice just before the fish. Add the fish to the tomato mixture and cook an additional 20 minutes. The fish should remain firm; if the pieces begin to break apart, turn off the heat to avoid overcooking.

 Add salt and pepper, to taste. Serve with a salad and fresh bread.

APPLE-BERRY CRISP

Greenlanders enjoy many different recipes using berries and apples. They are especially fond of crisp toppings. In this recipe we have added a few American touches to make it easier to follow. Makes 6 servings.

  3 cups apples, peeled and sliced thin
  2 cups fresh blueberries (not frozen)
  ⅓ cup water
  ¾ cup flour
  1 cup sugar
  ½ teaspoon cinnamon
  ¼ teaspoon salt
  ¼ pound butter, cut into small pieces
  1 cup heavy cream

Preheat oven to 350°F (176.67°C).

Butter a 1½-quart baking dish. Spread the berries and sliced apples in layers, and sprinkle the water over the top.

Combine flour, sugar, cinnamon, and salt in a mixing bowl. Rub the butter pieces into this mixture with your fingers until it resembles coarse crumbs. Spread this evenly over the apple-berry mixture. Bake for 40 minutes, or until the crust is brown.

Serve with heavy cream spooned on top.

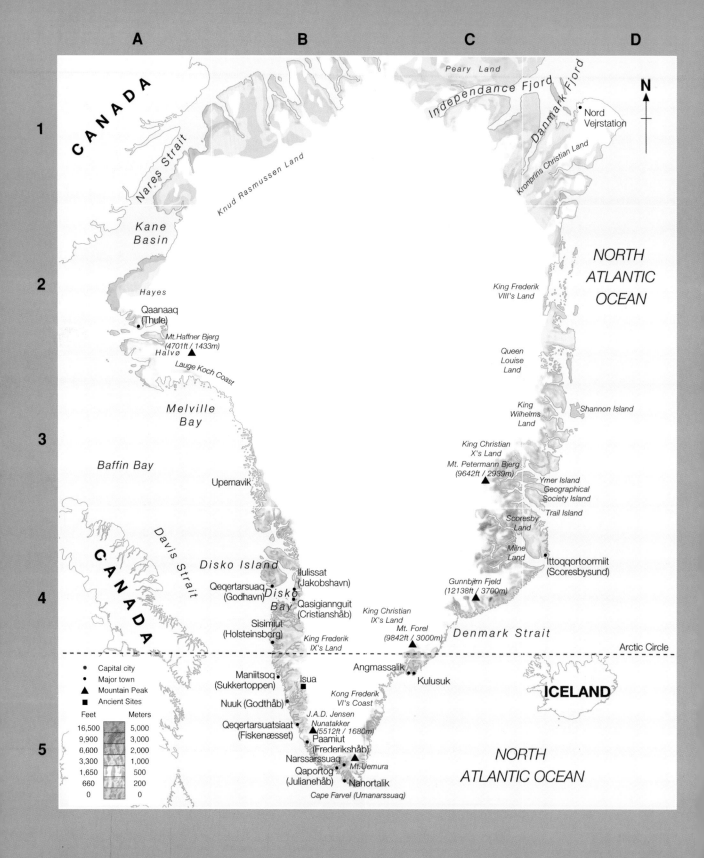

MAP OF GREENLAND

ECONOMIC GREENLAND

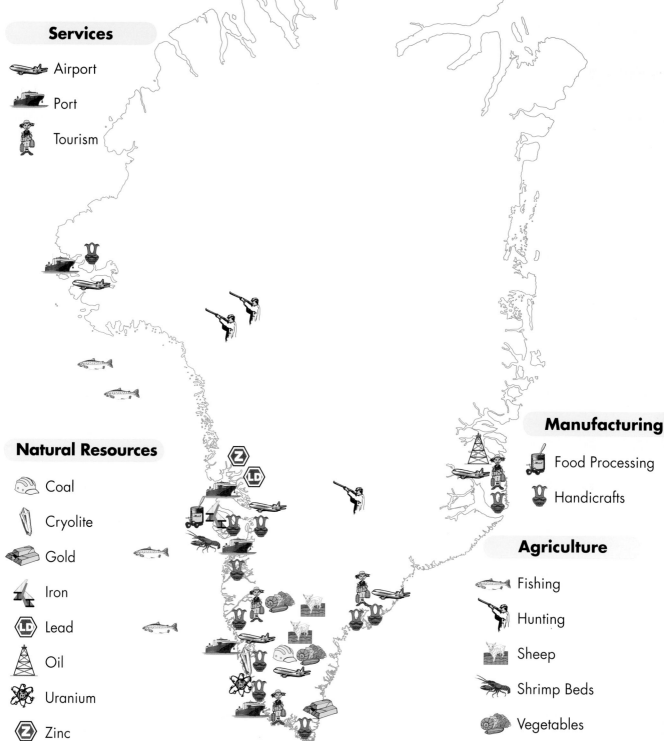

Services
- Airport
- Port
- Tourism

Natural Resources
- Coal
- Cryolite
- Gold
- Iron
- Lead
- Oil
- Uranium
- Zinc

Manufacturing
- Food Processing
- Handicrafts

Agriculture
- Fishing
- Hunting
- Sheep
- Shrimp Beds
- Vegetables

ABOUT THE ECONOMY

GROSS DOMESTIC PRODUCT (GDP)
2 percent (2007)

GDP SECTORS
NA

PER CAPITA INCOME
$443.57 (2006)

INFLATION RATE
2.3 percent (January 2006 to January 2007)

WORKFORCE
27,590 (born in Greenland)

UNEMPLOYMENT RATE
8.6 percent (2006)

POPULATION BELOW POVERTY LINE
NA

LAND AREA
839,999 sq mi (2,175,597 sq km)

ICE CAP
668,000 sq mi (1,730,000 sq km)

CURRENCY
Danish kroner; US $1 = Dkr 25

AGRICULTURAL PRODUCTS
Fishing: cod, halibut, shrimp, shellfish
Livestock: sheep, reindeer
Hunting: seal, caribou, musk ox
Farming: vegetables, hay

NATURAL RESOURCES
Gold, niobium, tantalite, iron, uranium, cryolite, zinc, copper coal

INDUSTRIES
Seafood processing (mainly halibut and shrimp), fishing, handcrafts, hides, small shipyards, mining

MAIN EXPORTS
Fish and fish products (87 percent)

MAIN IMPORTS
Machinery, transportation equipment, manufactured goods, petroleum products

MAJOR TRADE PARTNERS
Exports: Denmark, Japan, China
Imports: Denmark, Sweden, Ireland

CULTURAL GREENLAND

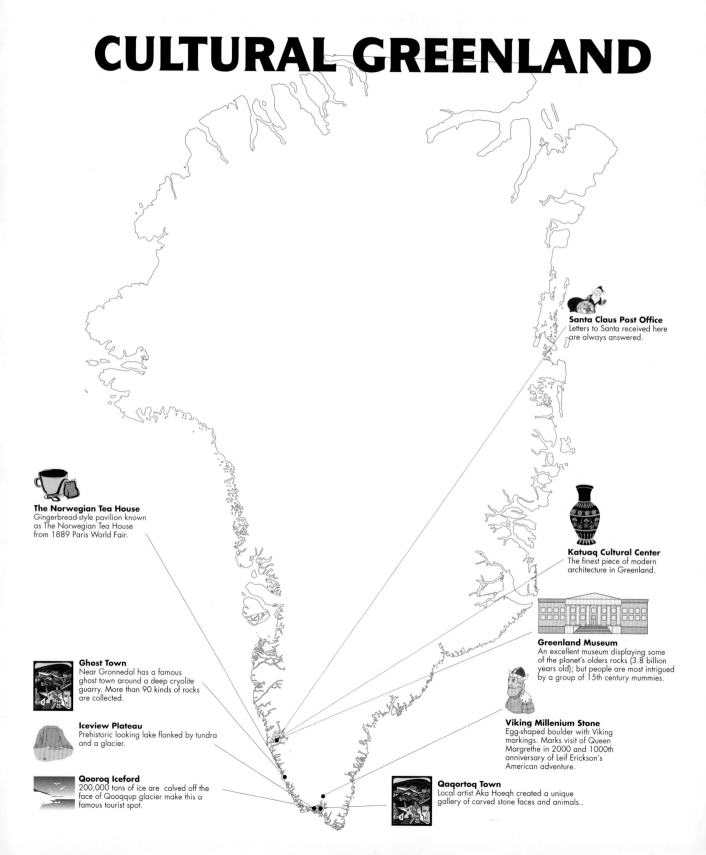

Santa Claus Post Office
Letters to Santa received here are always answered.

Katuaq Cultural Center
The finest piece of modern architecture in Greenland.

The Norwegian Tea House
Gingerbread-style pavilion known as The Norwegian Tea House from 1889 Paris World Fair.

Greenland Museum
An excellent museum displaying some of the planet's olders rocks (3.8 billion years old); but people are most intrigued by a group of 15th century mummies.

Ghost Town
Near Gronnedal has a famous ghost town around a deep cryolite quarry. More than 90 kinds of rocks are collected.

Iceview Plateau
Prehistoric looking lake flanked by tundra and a glacier.

Viking Millenium Stone
Egg-shaped boulder with Viking markings. Marks visit of Queen Margrethe in 2000 and 1000th anniversary of Leif Erickson's American adventure.

Qooroq Iceford
200,000 tons of ice are calved off the face of Qooqqup glacier make this a famous tourist spot.

Qaqortoq Town
Local artist Aka Hoeqh created a unique gallery of carved stone faces and animals..

ABOUT THE CULTURE

OFFICIAL NAME
Kalaallit Nunaat (Greenlandic, meaning "Land of the People") Gronland (Danish)

CAPITAL
Nuuk (Godthaab)

OTHER MAJOR TOWN
Qaqortoq; Ilulissat ("The Icebergs"); Kangerlussuaq; Sisimiut

FLAG
Designed by artist Thue Christiansen, adopted by the Home Rule Government in 1985. Two equal horizontal bands of white (top) and red (bottom), with a large disk placed slightly to the hoist side of center. The top half of the disk is red; the bottom half is white. In the top half of the flag the white represents the ice cap, and the red part of the circle indicates the fjords. In the lower half of the flag the red represents the ocean, while the white symbolizes the icebergs and the pack ice.

POPULATION
56,901 (January 2006)

POPULATION DENSITY
0.07 per square mile

LIFE EXPECTANCY
Female: 74 years; Male: 66 years (2007)

ETHNIC GROUPS
Inuit 89 percent; others, mostly Danish, 11 percent (Jan. 2006)

LANGUAGES
Greenlandic, Danish

NATIONAL HOLIDAYS
New Year's Day (January 1); Labor Day (May 1); National Day, Ullortuneq (Longest Day) (June 21); New Year's Eve (December 31, afternoon only)

LITERACY RATE
93 percent

TIME
Most of Greenland is three hours behind Greenwich Mean Time (GMT –0300).

FAMOUS GREELANDERS
Erik the Red established first Viking colony on Greenland; Pastor Hans Egede established the first Lutheran mission on Greenland in 1721; also founded the town of Godthaab ("Good Hope"), which became Nuuk, the island's largest town and capital; Knud Rasmussen, of Inuit and Danish ancestry, explorer and author; Aron and Cecilie Kleist, famous carvers of tupilak.; Aka Høegh, considered the greatest of Greenland's artists.

TIME LINE

IN GREENLAND	IN THE WORLD

c. 2400 B.C.
First Inuit migrate to Greenland from Canada.

1400 B.C.
Some Inuit tribes move into southern Greenland.

753 B.C.
Rome is founded.

116–17 B.C.
The Roman empire reaches its greatest extent, under Emperor Trajan (98–17 B.C.).

A.D. 600
Height of Mayan civilization

A.D. 900s
People of the Thule Culture arrive in Greenland from Alaska.

c. 930
Viking Gunnbjörn Ulfsson becomes the first European to see Greenland.

982
Erik the Red sails for Greenland.

985
Erik the Red leads a major settlement in Greenland.

1000
Leif Erikson becomes the first European to land on North American soil.

1000
The Chinese perfect gunpowder and begin to use it in warfare.

1261
Norway claims Greenland.

Late 1400s
Last Norse settlers mysteriously disappear.

1530
Beginning of transatlantic slave trade organized by the Portuguese in Africa.

1558–1603
Reign of Elizabeth I of England

1605
Denmark claims Greenland.

1620
Pilgrims sail the *Mayflower* to America.

1721
Missionary Hans Egede establishes a Lutheran mission at present-day Nuuk.

1774
Royal Greenlandic Trade Department establishes a trade monopoly for Denmark.

1776
U.S. Declaration of Independence

1789–99
The French Revolution

IN GREENLAND	IN THE WORLD
	1861 The U.S. Civil War begins.
	1869 The Suez Canal is opened.
1888 Norwegian explorer Fridtjof Nansen becomes the first European to cross Greenland's ice pack.	
1909 American Robert Peary mistakenly believes he has found the North Pole.	**1914** World War I begins.
	1939 World War II begins.
1940 Germany, under Hitler, occupies Denmark.	
1941 U.S. establishes air bases at Thule and two other locations.	
1942–1945 Greenlanders fight Germans for control of Greenland's weather stations.	**1945** The United States drops atomic bombs on Hiroshima and Nagasaki.
1953 Greenlanders become full citizens of Denmark.	**1949** The North Atlantic Treaty Organization (NATO) is formed.
1968 American B-52 bomber crashes near Thule, losing four nuclear bombs.	**1957** The Russians launch Sputnik.
	1966–69 The Chinese Cultural Revolution
1979 Home Rule is established.	
1985 Greenland withdraws from European Economic Community (EEC) but remains part of Denmark.	**1986** Nuclear disaster at Chernobyl in Ukraine
	1991 Breakup of the Soviet Union
	1997 Hong Kong is returned to China.
	2001 Terrorists crash planes in New York, Washington, D.C., and Pennsylvania.
2007–2009 International Polar Year involves study of global warming.	**2003** War in Iraq

GLOSSARY

anorak
A pullover jacket made of seal or caribou skin.

Arctic Palerfik
An annual three-day family dogsledding trip.

aurora borealis (or northern lights)
Dramatic ribbons of green and magenta produced when particles from the sun that collide with oxygen and hydrogen atoms in earth's upper atmosphere.

bergy bits
Small chunks of floating ice.

calving
The breaking off of ice from a large ice mass to form icebergs.

fjords
Steep-sided sea inlets that stretch far inland.

Greenlandic Iron Man Race
A grueling two-person five-day race.

Inughuit
The northernmost Inuit, also called the Polar Inuit or the Polar Eskimos.

Landsret
The high court of Greenland.

Landsstyre
The Home Rule cabinet that conducts the day-to-day business of the government.

Landstinget
Greenland's parliament.

pack ice
Sea ice that has thickened.

permafrost
Permanently frozen layer below the surface.

sea ice
Frozen seawater.

tidewater glaciers
Glaciers that flow into the sea.

tundra
Treeless plain in which only the top layer of soil thaws in the summer; allows a short growing season.

tupilak
Carved figures with grotesque features.

umiaks
Large, open boats, like kayaks but larger, made of tough sealskin and used for hunting seals and whales.

FURTHER INFORMATION

BOOKS

Howarth, David. *The Sledge Patrol.*New York: Lyons Press, 2001.

Malaurie, Jean. *Ultima Thule: Explorers and Natives in the Polar North*, translated by Willard Wood & Anthony Roberts. NY: W.W. Norton & Co., 2003.

O'Carroll, Etain and Mark Elliott. *Greenland and the Arctic.* Victoria, Australia: Lonely Planet Publications, 2005.

Rasmussen, Knud. *Across Arctic America*. Fairbanks: University of Alaska Press, 1927; reprinted 1999.

WEB SITES

Arctic Climate Impact Assessment (ACIA) www.acia.uaf.edu

North Pole Environmental Observatory Program http://psc.apl.washington.edu/northpole

Official Tourism and Business Council of Greenland www.greenland.com

Detailed information on territory of Nunavut www.nunavuttourism.com

BIBLIOGRAPHY

BOOKS

Anonymous. *The Vinland Sagas: The Norse Discovery of America.* Harmondsworth, UK: Penguin Books, 1965.

Dupre, Lonnie, ed. *Greenland Expedition: Where Ice is Born.* Minnetonka, MN: NorthWord Press, 2000.

Lopez, Barry. *Arctic Dreams.* New York: Random House, 1986.

Malaurie, Jean. *Ultima Thule: Explorers & Natives in the Polar North.* NY: W.W. Norton & Co., 2003.

O'Carroll, Etain and Mark Elliot. *Greenland and the Arctic.* Victoria, Australia: Lonely Planet Publications, 2005.

Rasmussen, Knud. *Across Arctic America.* Fairbanks: University of Alaska Press, 1927; reprinted 1999.

WEB SITES

Greenland National Museum and Archives. www.natmus.gl

Katuaq Cultural Center. www.katuaq.gl

Greenland Research Center. www.natmus.dk/sw18625.asp

INDEX